Brilliant Business Strategies for

P$YCHO SUCCESS

Mattox

PSYCHO SUCCESS

© 2012 by SW Strata

Published by
SW Strata
Dallas, Texas

FIRST EDITION

Printed in the U.S.A.

Cover design by Linsey Stiles

ISBN-13: 978-1-62620-520-8

www.PsychoSuccess.com

Acknowledgements

A special shout out to the below mentors who have motivated me, cultivated my skills, and galvanized my pursuits while demonstrating that success is achieved through ambition void of limits.

Bryan Barretto, Jay Dowling, Ken Good Jr., and Chris Tabor

A special thanks to God almighty for being so gracious to allow me to spend my remaining days with my beautiful wife Katy. Without her my life would be deprived of color.

Contents

Leading Off

This book will divulge some of the most exciting, cutting-edge strategies that deal makers, rainmakers and capitalists leverage every day to make their multimillion-dollar deals happen. I have seen all of these strategies and techniques firsthand during the last fifteen years of my life. I worked for corporate America, then struck out on my own to find financial success in several industries, including commercial real estate, small business and angel investing in growth companies. I have seen most management tools, styles, numerous types of organizations, fads and strategies poorly executed, and some executed to perfection, thus my interest in bringing these strategies to you, the reader.

Maybe you're not happy with the current state of your business or your life. Maybe that's why you picked up this book. In all honesty, the reason I wrote this book was due to my own unhappiness, knowing I needed a change. At one time in my personal and professional life—probably much like your own at some point—my existence (I, my 'being,' 'self') was in no real hurry to find its confidence, esteem, or true meaning, nor even motivated to push forward towards more [fill in the blank]. I was to the point where I simply didn't care. I had a good-paying corporate job with real security, since my managers seemed to like the work I did. I had just purchased a small home and really didn't have a care. But at a certain level I wanted more. Don't we all get like this?

I began to want more, but what was so wrong was that I wanted more of what other people had. I was not satisfied. I was not content. And I wished for what I couldn't have, nor afford. Not just more toys, more travel, more girlfriends or a Rockefeller house, but a sense of being somebody who had *more* than the guy in the next cubicle.

To be somebody, you do have to have more and do more of whatever *more* is. To get more is a hard-fought game, as more takes time to achieve. Neither you nor I have more time. Time is infinite, but *your* time is not. Time is the rarest of commodities, since one can't get more of it. You can't produce more time, barter for it, stretch it further, purchase it, steal it or save it. But we all yearn for more time. When you finally realize your time is coming to an end, what do you do? You go do what you've always wanted to, you get your affairs in order, you spend more time with the people who make your life worth living, and you make sure that everyone is taken care of prior to leaving this earth.

Live life with the same sense of urgency and without any waste, because you will never get this time back. Do you realize you are the youngest you are ever going to be and the oldest you have ever been? That said, stop watching the reality shows—hell, stop watching *television* altogether—and start *living* your own show. I'm no doctor, but you're on notice. Your time is coming to an end. Start living and leaving a legacy for a better you, a better life and a better world. Your clock is ticking...

With less waste, more time becomes available as you begin to slot other priorities to pursue where waste once was. I, like you, wanted to better myself, to be more efficient, to accomplish tasks faster, to give myself more time for all the items I needed to do to be somebody and to have much more of *more.* Much like many of us do at one time or another, I began to read motivational books, listen to CDs and attend get-rich-quick seminars. After a few of these, I realized that all these motivational speakers do is spew the same bullsh*t techniques and strategies, seminar after seminar and book after book, giving you and I no real value after reading your first motivational book or nothing you couldn't attain by just reading a couple of back issues of

INC. Magazine.

I call these ever-present techniques "shooting lay-ups." You'll find a few of these frequently-used strategies in the beginning of this book to retrench your memory, but only to be used as a baseline and recall some of the motivational foundations that we must all keep in mind. Don't worry, I picked the most important ones so as not to waste your time on the same old crap other motivational/inspirational books continue to throw against the wall.

Furthermore, as I test-marketed this book, I discovered that many people who have read several business/motivational books still find themselves mired in the stinking cesspool of underachievement. They need to be reminded of these basics because somewhere along the way they forgot to insert the bullet in the chamber. So I will cover them and thus set the foundation for *your* Psycho Success.

The majority of the chapters in this book are innovative techniques and thoughts to take your professional game from the expected to the significant. My mission for sharing my Psycho Success business strategies is to wake you up: to show you the direction to relevancy in your company or to twist your arm to follow your dreams and launch a business or vault your current company into the extraordinary.

I have been in all of these situations, and I know that you

are anxious to fight for more and to quickly become someone who has more. Understand, this book is nothing more than a collection of mere words. Words do not execute. Words do not turn off the television. Words don't get on the phone and seek opportunity. You do and you must, if you want more. I cannot execute these strategies for you, but I understand that your inspiration and your motivation are exceptional. *Psycho Success* is a short, laser-focused, quick-hitting read on strategies that have worked for me throughout my entire professional life. You will find them very useful and to the point, allowing you to achieve more.

CHAPTER ONE

Honey Badger Psychology

In the wilds of Africa, the honey badger is the most aggressive and fearless creature in the animal kingdom. While small in stature, the honey badger will scare off lions and jackals, chase down a king cobra, fight it mercilessly and shred a snake. And without a single ounce of fear, the honey badger will scale a tree to attack a hive of bees, oblivious to the enraged swarm buzzing around it as the badger casually savors the honey. Does the honey badger worry about getting bit or stung? No. It knows the rewards far exceed the risks. How would your life look if you lived like the Honey Badger, void of fear?

> Approach All Challenges with
>
> the Fearless Tenacity of the Honey Badger.

That said, it is not lost on this author how life can throw relentless issues at you. Life can be daunting at times. Loved ones get sick. Relationships are torn apart. Your business is DOA. Divorce is a real possibility. These types of dreadful experiences are hard to get your head around. But the overwhelming psychological belief is that you can never move past these experiences and that they can haunt you forever. In many cases, the same can be said for your financial existence. You are living with numerous dreadful experiences that have shaped your mindset that keep you from continuing to take calculated risks. You continue to feel the terror that those experiences might happen again. This is the paranoia of fear. That worry, that feeling of dread, is a great and horrible burden to bear. But the worst part is that this fear continually cripples you financially. At some point, fear can begin to consume your entire life and leave you paralyzed from the pursuit of your dreams. Fear is detrimental to you physically, emotionally, spiritually and financially. Fear feels tired. Fear is powerful. Fear squeezes tighter and tighter. Fear is crushing you. You feel the horror of fear. Isn't it time you stopped fearing fear?

Fear and fearful thoughts are massively damaging to your health, your relationships and certainly to your financial success. Fear interferes with sleep, with dreams, with desires, with hope and with personal progression. Fear leads to worry, and if you're a God-fearing individual, worry is a sinful act. In fact, the only real fear you should have is the fear of God. Period.

To live in fear is simply a rationalization of why you can't or couldn't make your goals a reality. Each day I see people use fear as a justification to keep themselves from experiencing failure, which leads to the even greater loss of financial independence. "I can't start a business because [insert some absurd excuse here]. Why even try?" Don't let fear be the justification of your financial position in life.

Certainly, other factors play a role, but I believe that fear plays the starring role. Stop living in fear and be accountable to yourself. I'm not suggesting that you ignore facts and take undue risks to get involved with pursuits you know little about. What I *am* suggesting is that you can't let fear be the driving force in your financial decisions and the horror that restrains you from taking risks for financial rewards.

Fear is Self-Created

and Entirely Unnecessary.

With fear you feel anger nonstop. Fear raises your hostility and animosity towards life. Fear seizes your true greatness. Fear evokes excuses, and excuses don't care about you or your goals. Yet excuses seem to be everywhere. You should have no excuses. None. Hell, the real fear should be of falling behind in your personal financial growth and/or your competitor out-executing you. Fear defeats your potential. Fear is binding. Imagine where you would be without fear.

Recalibrate your fearful thoughts and turn your fear into a positive force. When you learn to live with fear, understand the fear and appreciate the fear. Fear can drive you to accomplish beyond your self-imposed limits. Fear should compel you to something greater. Fear can and *will* supply you the physical and emotional energy that will catapult you past your potential. The fact is, fear should piss you off and provide the adrenaline to start conquering your past fears and living abundantly. Live in the present. Quit with all of the excuses and use the power of fear to drive achievement through the terror of NOT realizing your goals.

When I look back at some of the experiences, fears and excuses I've had—and a few I still need to conquer—I'm reminded of a sermon my pastor once delivered the Sunday right after New Year's Day. He told the congregation that the God of Opportunity and Hope only gets angry when we make excuses.

Let that sink in for a moment. Seriously, of all the possibilities in life that could cause the Higher Power to become angry with you, the individual God personified is not only disappointed but also repulsed by excuses through the embodiment of fear. That is profound, isn't it?

The pastor went on to tell this fantastic story about a very stressful time in his life when he was a young college coach and not yet a minister. He knew he should be working out, not only to help with the coaching stress, but for his health in general. He was never a morning person, so for a New Year's resolution he decided to start waking up early and working out. To accomplish this, he would have to drive to a fitness center to begin morning workouts. When he arrived the first morning, he thought that it was way too early to be there. "Why am I doing this?" he said to himself. "I can come back at 10 a.m. when I'll have more energy." Mistake #1: He was allowing a lame excuse to derail his mission. He wasn't approaching his workout like a tenacious honey badger.

So he pulled out of his spot and drove to the edge of the parking lot. He sat idle for a moment, while his desire to go home and back to bed played tug-of-war with his mission to exercise. He looked back at the fitness center. "Well, I'm here. I might as well go in." He wheeled the car back around and parked out front only to let another excuse take over his mind. So he drove off and again stopped at the edge of the parking lot.

He was about to turn on to the highway when he said to himself, "Okay, let's just do a few exercises and go home." So he returned to the center. He got out of the car, walked into the gym, and the first person to greet him with a clipboard became his wife of fifteen years and the mother to his three children.

> # Take Action without Fear
> # and Let the Rewards Commence.

Lastly, get excited about life! Be excited about the opportunities you have. You know what you were meant for. Don't fear the fear; embrace the fear. Let the fear fuel the passion inside. Everyone always overestimates the downside risk. Don't be that person. Make things happen. Kick yourself in the ass. Be your harshest critic. And put Carpe Diem at the forefront of your life. Psycho Success is about taking on the honey badger's psychology and pursuing life relentlessly, void of fear. Hell, the animal is known to slay cobras. Isn't it time you take the anxiety of fear out of your life?

CHAPTER TWO

Shooting Lay-ups

Let's begin with the basics that you've probably seen in many other business/motivational books, but need to be reinforced. Hence the name "Shooting Lay-ups."

What are the basic skills or the easy lay-ups, if you will?

Strategize, Focus and Execute.

All of your skills are critical to success, but these three—strategizing, focusing and executing—are the keys to your ultimate financial goals. As to choosing the most important skill, General George Patton said it best, "A good plan, violently executed now, is better than a perfect plan next week." The key word here is *execution*. The plan doesn't have to be absolutely perfect, but must be executed violently and with great fervor. With life, with business and with the tools in this book, you will learn how to execute violently.

Speaking of execution, I ran into a business owner who had numerous grandiose, moneymaking ideas and schemes. Some were genius, some ridiculous, but unfortunately he hated dealing with people. Nor did he like keeping up with schedules, and organization in general was a real challenge. He was making decent money, mostly from his off-the-chart ideas that his friends would run with and cut him in on, but only for a small percentage. I told him he needed to find an *executioner*, someone he could hire as COO to execute his crazy ideas through his own company. He ultimately took the advice and, in less than two years, became a multimillionaire, all because his organization suddenly valued execution over the idea.

He realized that a person with brilliant ideas but no ability to execute is simply a lunatic. With someone to execute those ideas, suddenly he's a genius! The thin line between being a lunatic and a genius is labeled "Execution." No amount of strategies or tradecraft will help you without the motivation and execution.

Sometimes You Play the Man,

Not the Negotiation.

Now with that said, don't think for a moment that you can walk into a meeting ten minutes before go-time without any planning and be successful solely by executing to your fullest extent. Professional businessmen today thrive on unprepared owners, negotiators and brokers. These are the chum on which the professional sharks feed. That's why you need a plan, a strategy and better tactics. Even General Patton understood that violent execution is not possible without a great strategy.

Your starting point in the tradecraft of negotiation is that your strategy needs to be extremely well thought out, and you must always be two steps ahead of your competition. You need to reach the understanding that your competition has strategized, schemed and is focused like a laser on kicking your everloving ass to get everything they want from the negotiation. You need to know the important deal points your competition finds attractive, and then leverage those points to offer more options that appeal to the man sitting across the table from you, but which ultimately get you across your goal line faster. Here are five key steps you need to take before your business meeting, negotiation or sales presentation.

1. Take some quiet time and turn off your cell phone, iPad, etc. and think about exactly what you want to accomplish. Write the goals down, but know them cold. Think about solutions.

2. Organize the list of goals into priorities, beginning with the most important. These are your goals or objectives.

3. Take some serious time to analyze your opponent. Put yourself in his shoes. What is his agenda? What are his goals and objectives? During this process, assume he has no conscience, as he rarely will. When you do that, I promise you, his perspective will soon become apparent. Then you will begin to see the different tactics he might use to counter your positions. Write them down and keep them handy. Sometimes you have to play the man, not the negotiation.

4. Knowing all the perspectives, positions and possible tactics as well as your opposing party does allows you to brainstorm about the negotiation. Use this session and knowledge to your advantage. Think of it as strategizing about how you would kick your own ass if you were on the other side of the table. The light bulb *will* suddenly go off on where

the opposing party will try to attack your positions or you personally.

5. When you negotiate, convey the conflict and positions between the two parties. Create options by juxtaposing where the parties are with where they could be. Describe the deal, as the opposing party knows it, so that he knows you recognize his issues and stance. This should create a bond and open your opposition up to hearing your ideas. After you set that baseline, introduce your ideas of what could be. This is a good starting point to finding deal points that can be agreed upon. Through your research you should know where you can give and where you can't.

I have found that if you quickly answer all of the opposing party's negotiation questions with good strong answers or counter-questions, he will realize that he needs to pull out his BAFO (Best and Final Offer). And if that's not good enough, *always* be prepared to slide your chair back from the table, stand up and walk away. Be bold when negotiating deals.

> **Bold Understands When to Take the Deal and When to Walk.**

Wealthy clients constantly tell me stories of their best deals, but most of the time when pressed, their best deals are the ones that they never did. If you walk away, don't be surprised if the next day you get a phone call from the other party wishing to renegotiate. Sometimes this process takes weeks or months, but most of the time you will get another call. They may tell you to go suck it again, but it's usually a cordial call.

By taking the time to plan, you can avoid being that guy who looks around the table and can't find the greater fool. It's the same in marketing as it is in negotiating deals. You must always be pushing the edge and operating in the grey. That's where the ridiculously untapped Psycho Success lies. Push before you are moved. And move before you are pushed. Know the angles. Know the market. Know the players and locate your company's white space.

Bold Is the Lightning Rod

That Operates in the Grey.

Step outside yourself for a better perspective and take a good long look. Try looking from a fresh perspective, not your client's or an opponent's perspective. Consider someone from another industry. They may bring to light an idea, which you have yet to consider. In their industry there is an entirely different view, a different language and different goals. But the ultimate goal remains the same, and almost always you can find something to take from their industry to help you in yours.

For example, my clients in commercial real estate. I have asked them all to take credit cards. Why? Because they provide great benefits for not only the client/tenant, but for the landlord as well. Credit cards are easy to work with. You get paid regularly instead of waiting on the mail. Plus, you rack up a tremendous amount of miles or points. Credit cards are an important way, and an easy way, of doing business. Be easy to do business with. Think of how many startups you know that began with debt from credit cards.

Very often I see the inappropriate focus on trends and ridiculous processes rather than on profits. It is not lost on me that it is a mountain of a task to run a company. You must lead, motivate, train, listen, create, monitor, sell, etc. to make an organization operate efficiently. But understand, less profitable companies sink into mediocrity, because these companies lack the absolute commitment to be determined and to be tough on processes and costs that take away from focusing on the bottom line. Most business owners or managers are afraid of aggressively cutting costs because they might be considered vicious or petty. Get over it. If you're good at what you do, this is a fear unfounded.

Embrace Fear and Make It Your Bitch.

You must have the resolve to lead your organization with what is consistent to the recommendations in this book, not just the lay-ups in these early chapters. Don't get depressed if you failed to close the deal and cash flow is going in the wrong direction. Don't worry. Learn from it and look at it as an opportunity. Focus on the next goal, strategize and move ahead with even better execution.

CHAPTER THREE

Bold Is the New Awesome!

The World Needs Bold. You need bold. You need more of bold to move your career or company forward and execute on the strategies in this book. But further, with this book I am sharing many ways you can go beyond the usual limits of conventional thinking and creativity and advance your current being into becoming a much more sophisticated person. Throughout this book, I recommend taking mental notes of where you could use these highly developed techniques in your workplace. As you read each of the strategies, imagine the unique ways you could use them to achieve the success you deserve. To me, it all starts with being bold. Bold will change your life.

And to hammer home just how important it is for you to be bold in everything you do, let me run through a spitball session of what Bold is and why Bold will make you more effective in your business and career.

Bold doesn't just show up, it speaks up. It stands up. Bold is present. Bold is market-facing. Bold is relevant in whatever conversation it has with clients, employees or vendors. Bold adds value. Bold does not shoot lay-ups. Bold is on point. Bold is certain it understands. Bold speaks confidently. Bold is comfortable with the concept of which it speaks. Bold doesn't back down from what it knows to be correct. Bold is beginning to change you.

Bold is always bullish. People follow Bold. Leadership rewards Bold. Bold is self-determined. Bold is not lazy, nor does it phone it in. Bold is not Bush League. Bold likes the heavy lifting and takes up the slack when others won't. Bold takes ownership when needed. Bold pulls more than Bold's share. And Bold produces. Bold is flat out better.

Bold promotes itself. Bold takes calculated risks. Risk embraces Bold. Bold is creativity embodied. Bold is a contrarian that perceives differently and never drinks the Kool-Aid. Bold thinks and operates on another level. Bold is always a step ahead. Bold goes right when others go left because Bold has a roadmap. Bold always feels his back is against the wall. Bold gets results, maybe not always the ones intended, but people, clients and the public never forget Bold. Never forget Bold. Bold doesn't believe in lead balloons. Bold is entrepreneurial and does not apologize for being Bold.

Bold educates itself and becomes an expert in its field. Bold challenge others, but challenges itself far more. Bold imagines the future and finds the blue sky. Bold does not wait for a post mortem. Bold understands what it has to do. Bold does not piss in the ocean, because Bold has Bold goals. Bold waits for no one. And others can't wait for Bold to happen. Bold nuts up, and by reading this book, it understands where Bold can take anyone. Why not be Bold?

Bold is the lightning rod that operates in the grey. Bold understands why it must. Bold is always locked and loaded. Bold relies on leverage and uses its resources. Bold is influence. Bold knows where the line is. And Bold understands why not to cross it. Bold respects common sense, but Bold sometimes demands justification. Bold makes good arguments in the face of lesser ones. Bold understands push back, but Bold pushes harder. Bold sells Bold. And there is plenty of commerce. Are you a buyer?

Bold cannot worry about what others think, nor can Bold care. Hell, some of the most successful businesses were laughed at for being so Bold. Bold is not out for a quick win. Bold knows its place and it is on top. Bold operates at all pay grades and Bold is on a mission. Bold is spectacular. Bold is a game changer. Bold is empty of fear and Bold is handsomely rewarded. Are you Bold?

CHAPTER FOUR

Enjoy the Silence

Listening is a critical skill in the game of business. What is unfortunate is that it is tragically underutilized. That's because you are talking all the time. You never shut up. You talk day and night, hour to hour. Do you really believe you have so much fantastic information and value that the person you are talking with wants to hear all your brain drain dribble? If you're not this type of person, great. But chances are you've been on the phone with this type; you could set the phone down and come back an hour later only to hear them still yapping away about their phenomenal life experiences.

If you are one of *those* people, see if this fits. When you are with a client or negotiating a deal, you love the control and sense of power, authority and strength it brings. So you insist on complete command of the sales pitch, conference call, meeting or negotiation. Understand, the more you talk, the more additional information you reveal about your position, your tactics and your BAFO. Many times, before they can even accept your initial offer, you plow ahead and present a better deal. You are your own worst enemy.

To perform all this talking, you've worked on your breathing. Your lungs are worthy of a gold medal swimmer or a pearl diver searching the ocean floor without oxygen tanks. You are able to talk for hours while taking only a few breaths. Like the mindless pundits on TV, you have trained yourself to take a breath in the middle of a sentence rather than at the end, because you know you will not be interrupted that way.

Nervous and insecure people talk when there is unexpected silence. It makes them uncomfortable, so to fill this silence they give up all kinds of interesting topics of conversation. They will often divulge personal facts that they wouldn't dare express otherwise. Another kind of person who fills the silence gaps is a control freak. He or she will grab the steering wheel simply because no one is steering. They cannot stand for someone not to have their hands on the wheel. It's freaky. You know these people. You've talked to them. Heard them jabber nonstop just to fill the silence with unnecessary words. You do not want to be these people. Use silence to your advantage. Enjoy the silence and thrive in the silence.

Are you nervous, insecure or a control freak? If you are, there are sharks waiting to take advantage of talkative guppies. Don't be a guppy. Who are these sharks that take advantage of all this talking by sitting and listening to adversaries who spill their guts? Police officers. The Mafia. Judges. Millionaires. Clients. All are happy to hand you the knife and watch as you slit your own throat.

If you make an offer, go silent and wait for their response. Don't worry if it takes two minutes without anyone talking. Just sit there and focus on breathing slowly. Think positive thoughts. Typically, the opponent will think it's so awkward that they will say something, maybe taking the deal or maybe revealing vulnerability.

You've put *Bold* out there, now close your mouth.

CHAPTER FIVE

Relentless Pursuit

Each time you get in your car you are going somewhere with a goal in mind. If you are driving aimlessly then you are stoned, lost or glad to be out of jail. It's good to have goals. Every single business and motivational book out there mentions goal setting. Some hammer the concept at you with every page. I'm not going to, but to be a psycho dealmaker and marketer you must have specific goals and the priority goal of *profit*.

It's very hard to grasp where you are going and how to get there without any real thought as to what your goals are in life. Goals help you visualize what your life will look like years later. Write your goals down on a regular basis, even as they morph into different aspirations. I have my goals pinned up in list-form next to my desk. These bad boys stare me in the face daily, giving me a purpose to fuel my ambition. Many times, your goals do not include becoming wealthy or being successful professionally. If that's the case, you, my friend, are reading the wrong book. Please walk over and hand it to someone who actually has high ambitions.

Your first goal and number one priority in business is to make a profit. If you can't make a profit then you're in the wrong profession or the wrong business. It may take a substantial amount of time to make money, but the goal of profit has a permanent place atop your list. Nothing else in business matters if you can't accomplish your #1 goal.

Understand, it's always about the bottom line, *not* top line revenue. I see a good amount of confusion in business over goal prioritization. People often forget that the purpose of their business is to make money, not to simply keep growing the business without the objective of profit. A company's life span is too short to focus on anything but making a profit. If you're not making money after a certain period of time and your burn rate is bringing available cash to an end, this is called a hobby. If you have a smile on your face when you realize this, please go hug more trees, or ride in the rubber speedboat chasing whalers in the Atlantic.

In your company, I believe the following communication should be drilled into every employee: (1) We are here to make a profit. (2) All revenue taken in by this organization will focus on realizing our potential as a company and to make even more profit. We will relentlessly and aggressively pursue all avenues to accomplish this end. (3) We have massive untapped opportunities left to capture. (4) We are a profit-focused company and an incredibly exciting place to work. (5) All non-strategic expenses will be cut to the bone, resulting in a more streamlined and profitable company.

If you, the leader of your team or your company, execute this attitude and these actions towards profit, it will attract like-minded employees and business partners. And your goal of being profitable will be much easier and more quickly realized.

Instead of communicating to a subordinate about what you expect from them, you are communicating to yourself about what you expect from you. And your first communication should always begin with: make a profit. Never apologize to anyone for making a profit.

Bold Takes Calculated Risks

and Risk Embraces Bold.

Actually, your second goal should be to make as much profit as possible. Have goals, write your goals down and make profit a priority. Go out with relentless pursuit and make as much profit as possible.

CHAPTER SIX

Tomorrow Is an Excuse

Your mother has been kidnapped and the thugs insist that you perform a complex series of tasks to set her free. How quickly would you work to save your mother's life? You would have an extreme sense of urgency. This type of urgency needs to be present in all that you do for your business or department, as your competition wants to kick your ass 24/7. In today's connected world, things can happen incredibly fast. The next big thing is always around the corner and then a few years later —*poof*—it's irrelevant. The competition outworked, outsmarted and outproduced you because they were hungry and worked with a high sense of urgency. Where is MySpace or AOL today? I'll tell you where, in the slow lane.

You must be a leader and instill that same sense of urgency in those who work for you. Time really is money. Forget the excuses. We all hate excuses. Wake up each day and first conquer the tasks that directly lead to more revenue. Next, with a sense of urgency, perform the tasks on your to-do list that lead to a more efficient business and items that drive costs down or, preferably, completely eliminate them.

Typically, delaying a task or decision is not acting with a sense of urgency, but be careful. At times, waiting can be beneficial. Maybe you need to wait for certain market forces to resolve themselves or maybe a client cannot see you immediately. These are understandable, but procrastination is a bad thing. This vile word relates to tasks that need to be performed and decisions that need to be made; yet you simply push them aside to play *Call of Duty* during the afternoon. If this behavior is typical let me introduce you to failure.

Repetitive daily failures will begin to devour you and your company, making you less and less competitive until you're MySpace cowering in the shadows of Facebook and Twitter. I often see a tendency to procrastinate on critical business decisions due to uncertainty, instead of powering through analysis and gut instinct for a decisive conclusion. This is urgency. If the decision results in a failure, fail fast. Learn from your mistake and move on. Embrace this habit of following your gut through calculated risk and you'll begin to pin your ears back, bear down and power through your procrastination while insisting on a company culture that continually produces a sense of urgency that leads, not follows.

Meetings are another key area where people lack a sense of urgency. Most attendees are late and still talking on the phone when they stroll into the conference room. The rest of the team members probably have no idea why the meeting was called or what needs to be accomplished. Fix this! If the meeting starts at 3:00 then it starts at 3:00. Not 3:01 or 3:10. This sends a message where an urgency and importance will arise that says, "We are not meeting to *discuss*. We are meeting to *decide*." Sure a discussion needs to happen, but a decision must be reached, or valuable time and resources are being wasted. Meetings are like surgery: get in, evaluate, labor and get out quickly.

> ## Bold Does Not Wait for a Post Mortem.

Everyone respects and admires people who go out and take it. Does anyone respect the person who sits behind a desk and constantly watches his Facebook feed? Personally, you need to have a sense of urgency to succeed in today's expeditious business environment, but integrating and developing this urgency into your business is a real key to Psycho Success.

CHAPTER SEVEN

Hope and Grind

It's dangerous not to believe in a Higher Power. In fact, it's brainless. The earth has numerous natural laws which manage our planet and just happen to govern the galaxy and, by extension, our universe. Ask yourself, if all of this is random and pure chaos, why do these laws apply everywhere? In fact, why do we have laws at all? You see, laws denote order. Order means intelligence is at work. Personally, I believe in the Lord Jesus Christ, because without him I have zero hope in my life. I would encourage everyone to consider trusting in Christ for eternal salvation.

That said, whatever Higher Power you believe in or worship, I'm sure spirituality is the same for you. Spirituality gives us the momentum and the dose of hope we so desperately need in our lives. It helps people like us get up off the mat and be able to take another punch. If you have no hope of a better existence, then why grind through each day? We all hope for something more, and spirituality is that engine behind the energy called the human spirit. As you explore this subject more, you will begin to understand the deeper meaning and perhaps discover a new higher calling in your life.

For me, I know that faith has brought me through some dark times in my life. It can do the same for you too. Be bold and give spirituality a shot. You'll walk away amazed and, like me, addicted to the hope that only a Higher Power can bring.

CHAPTER EIGHT

Think Big, Then Go 10x

Think Big. If you're an entrepreneur or you are in a business of any kind, you have heard this oversold phrase. But it's one that rings true. You don't take a knife to a gunfight, and business is the same way. Bigger or scale is always an advantage in business.

Thinking big broadens your perspective and allows you to see many more opportunities or where the white space is for your business. Big thoughts encourage big ideas that make Psycho Success possible, if not probable. You will be reminded throughout your career that successful people visualize big ideas; it is one of the keys to their financial success. Most leaders recognize the need to think strategically about the future. But many fail to dedicate the proper time and attention to thinking about going big. Thinking about the big picture is not as simple as clearing your calendar and turning off your devices. When you make it a priority, you'll find that clearing your mind without distractions can begin to fill the white space with all types of ideas. Why is it that even the most ridiculous ideas sometimes find their way into the mainstream? Someone went big with his or her thought process. Sometimes even the most practical ideas are missed because someone didn't find the time to think on a broad scale.

Consider the broker who could put the same amount of work into a $400,000 deal as he could into a $2,000,000 deal. Yet the return on investment for his time is much better with the $2,000,000 deal. Some would say this is an opportunity cost issue and that would be correct. But it also suggests that the broker going after the $2,000,000 deal is looking at the 40,000-foot view and thinking bigger. The larger the vision, the bigger the results and the greater potential for superior financial success. Sounds like common sense, but you'd be surprised.

Bold Does Not Piss in the Ocean,

Because Bold Has Bold Goals.

Big ideas that lead to Psycho Success also come from whom you talk to. When you think big you must go to the top of the organization and speak with the man in the corner office. Many people fall short here as fear takes over. The perceived ass-chewing that may occur during a conversation with an executive paralyzes people from this action. I am continually surprised how much more the top of the organization is willing to speak with you than the bottom levels. This dynamic never ceases to amaze me. That is why bold people with big visions climb further up the food chain faster. Vision can be impressive when expressed correctly and coupled with an employee who lacks the fear of rejection. They are like the badass Dirty Harry, but instead of taking a .44 magnum into meetings, they bring their bold confidence with their bold ideas and dare you to "make their day." Going bigger than others will always produce far better results. Make it one of your arrows in your quiver.

CHAPTER NINE

Know Thy Numbers

Know your numbers cold and identify where your business stands financially on a day-to-day basis. Most successful people have a technology dashboard they look at every day to understand whether or not their online strategies are propelling them forward. This daily feedback is essential to making proper decisions. Do you think a pilot needs to know his numbers while flying a commercial airliner? Your business is the same way; it needs to know any number of metrics to understand where the opportunities are or where it can get better. Not knowing your numbers can mean a slow death for your business. And what's worse is you won't even see it coming.

To know your numbers cold you must understand how to read financial statements. If you don't fully understand how to read financial statements, pick up a *Financial Statements for Dummies* book if you have to. Do some homework and get educated.

Each day you need to understand the financial position of your business to know if you're really making any money. As time passes you can move to a weekly report or, after several years of experience, a monthly report. Each deal you do contains numbers and you must understand them to know if each deal or transaction is turning a profit. And there are a large variety of numbers, calculations and analytics you can use to analyze your business dealings. The point is to make sure you have all the right information for each deal in order to know if you are making a profit for your business. If you're not making a profit on a deal, is it really worth your time?

Bold Is Always Locked and Loaded.

Here are some tips I use: Let's start with the balance sheet. Think of a balance sheet as a thermometer that provides a quick look at the health of your business. You can quickly determine a business's solvency by checking its current assets. Which assets can be quickly converted to cash? These are the most important. What are the current liabilities or debts that need to be paid in the near future? Typically, the time frame for this is less than one year. Then examine the ratio between current assets and debts. If the ratio is less than one, the business could be in real trouble. If you are doing a deal and can look at the opposing company's balance sheet, a quick check of this ratio can give you a picture of their solvency which, if bad, you can then leverage in negotiations if need be. Whatever your business is, if the ratio is at one or below, you have to create wiggle room by postponing the payment of bills and speeding up the collection of receivables. This should keep the business afloat. Remember, cash and profit are not the same. If you run out of cash, like fuel to a pilot, you are out of business.

The other two main financial statement tools are the income statement and the cash flow statement. Notice what both of these focus on: cash. The income statement is a record of how much money the business has made or lost. The cash flow statement simply shows where the money is being spent, like a checkbook register. It all comes back to cash. And cash is typically an enormous issue in growing companies. When the employees don't get paid, the business flatlines. Always remember that numbers run companies. It is your responsibility as an owner to get the correct numbers in front of you, interpret the financial statements properly and realize how they can help you stay out of trouble or be more profitable.

CHAPTER TEN

Tap into Your Warehouse

Unless you were born a genius and have hundreds of creative ways to improve your business and make money, you're going to need others to help you come up with new and fresh ideas. That means it's your job to foster innovation throughout the business. To accomplish that, you have to enable people with the confidence to come up with crazy suggestions without fear of being ridiculed. The second you laugh at or make fun of their conceptual idea, you're dead; you've lost all credibility. When that happens you can expect no new ideas from that employee, and likely others as well. This feeling spreads among the employees like a sickness, and you are left with zombie employees just coming to work and going through the motions. They'll shut down and you will never get them back.

Part of your job is to train employees on the company. A

percentage of that training should teach that no matter their position, every employee's job is to understand the big picture. Knowing how the business operates and fits together is a key piece of knowledge that turns your business from a room full of mindless robots into go-big, creative machines. Any employee that has been in a position for a few months can tell you where inefficiencies exist, and thus how to improve productivity or perhaps how to better serve the client. Tapping into that warehouse of employee knowledge is not only your job, but crucial to achieving Psycho Success.

CHAPTER ELEVEN

The Angle of Value

Here's a new one: add value to your client's business. This is an easy lay-up for people who have been alive for the last 100 years. All idiots know this concept; so don't tell people what they already know. Step up and describe new innovative concepts with fresh information that only an expert like yourself would recognize. Of course, this requires you to have fresh information and to learn about new concepts. Meaning you have to be on top of your game about not only your business, but also your client's business. But you knew that.

> **Bold Educates Itself**
>
> **in the Industry of Its Clients.**

Take the very sexy business of mufflers. If you sell to muffler shops, how well do you know their business? How do they capture market share? New customers? What are the market demographics for the industry? For the local area? What about competitors? Devote some time to Internet research and you will learn a ton about muffler shops and the way they typically operate. By looking up muffler businesses for sale, you can read a lot about their business models. The next time you call on one, you will know enough to talk intelligently about their business and realize that they may not have time to keep up on the latest innovations in advertising or other new demographics that could boost their revenues. Combine those concepts with good, disruptive conceptual ideas that would improve their business and you become more valuable to their organization. But you knew that too.

Only when you fully understand your business can you show your client how to improve their business. For example, their product or service can likely be used for more than one purpose. This is such a disruptive way of thinking that the gears in your mind will continue to spin even after you have found other ways to market your client's product. If their company manufactures dog food to sell to veterinarians, you may discover that perhaps with other minor modifications they can sell their food to emergency relief centers for human consumption. If that's the case, you have just opened up new markets for your client. Or it may have nothing to do with dog food, but instead suggest a new contact to your client for a cheaper credit card processing firm, thereby lowering their processing fees. If you make your clients money, not only will they stay in business with your company, but your revenue will soar.

Disruptive thinking, not only in your business but also in your clients' businesses, is what will continue to create value and drive revenue for all parties, opening up new streams of revenue to achieve Psycho Success.

CHAPTER TWELVE

Be Locked In

If I gave you a choice between receiving ten grand in cash or a guaranteed prediction on which direction the price of gold would go the next day, which would choose? The $10,000 choice is tempting but limited. The gold prediction is virtually unlimited because with some clever investing, you could make millions from it. Its potential is infinite. And that's the difference between money and information. Information can allow you to make vast sums of money. Once you realize the value of information, you will want more of it.

Every day, undercover agents gather intelligence and pass it up the chain to analysts who make sense of all the data. In today's world, targeted publications and the Internet can give you the same information on your customers without having to resort to your own network of spies. Sure this information is available to everyone, but you can gain an advantage by being among the first to read local business journals, newspapers, trade publications and hard-to-find, industry-specific newsletters. Spend time scouring these sources for relevant leads, announcements of new businesses or industry news in general. To be first to the information is a huge competitive advantage. Wake up early and be the first to contact the pertinent people in these applicable stories. Top salespeople constantly tell me they consistently acquire new business by being the first to the information and the first on the phone.

Much of these sources have moved online, where you can type in keywords and search instantly for related leads. You can even set up alerts through Google that can scour the Internet daily and locate particular information, sending it directly to your inbox in real time. Start thinking in terms of combat. It is crucial that you get to the information—*and act upon it*—before your competition does. Then you need to quickly move your ass to take advantage of the information.

CHAPTER THIRTEEN

What Sucks!

You know what sucks: long-term projects. They weigh on you physically and mentally, draining you week after week while they remain unfinished. Long-term projects are obviously important, but employees tend to put them off to the last moment, torturing themselves for months. Employees must make these projects a priority and continue to make progress on them over the course of a project's lifespan.

What sucks even more is that typically the employee is stuck waiting on a team member to finish their part of the project before starting their own. Employees must learn that if they are to make long-term projects a priority, they must dumb down their goals. If one has too many goals, larger long-term projects will typically remain undone.

We find that breaking up the project into digestible pieces is the easiest way to manage a long-term project. Reminding co-workers of their responsibilities also helps, since they often forget, thus impacting the project's execution. Sending a friendly reminder is usually appreciated when someone is carrying a heavier workload. If the co-worker doesn't like a friendly nudge, make sure you cover your ass and copy your boss on the subsequent nudge.

The best way to keep employees on target with long-term projects is to make sure the employee adds the events to their calendar on a recurring basis. If an employee continues to see the event on his calendar, smaller, more manageable pieces will continue to be finished until the project is finally completed.

From your perspective, the owner/manager needs to make sure the employee has all the necessary tools, information, skill set and support system in place. If not, they will use the lack of any of those resources as the reason why the goal or project was not completed. Don't be that boss. Be the boss who understands what the project is going to require and ensure that access to those resources is uninhibited. What doesn't suck is bringing in a project on time, on budget, and pushing your business forward.

CHAPTER FOURTEEN

Birthing New Ideas

It is crucial. Let me say this again: it is crucial to have someone in the same industry to bounce ideas off of, network with
and to seek answers from to your most pressing business issues
and/or questions. Typically, these are seasoned veterans of the
industry. But today, younger, experienced entrepreneurs are becoming veterans very quickly.

A good mentor should provide you with a roadmap to
follow and help you overcome your fear of powering through
unfamiliar situations. A mentor will listen to and expand on
your ideas, giving you more confidence, and allowing you to
grow your knowledge base. Having a mentor is mandatory to
reaching your financial potential.

Look for mentors among your industry's associations, upper
level management and retired or active industry executives. You

want someone whom you respect, someone who has been in similar situations and understands your deal landscape. More often than not, the mentor benefits as much or more from your fresh perspective and from the personal satisfaction that someone is birthing their ideas throughout the industry they love.

You can have several mentors throughout life, and some won't be strictly business related. Some mentors will be spread all through your personal life, helping with relationships, physical fitness, alternative investments and other action-rich areas of your life. Your group of gurus will only enhance your capabilities, inspire boldness and remove the excuses of why an idea or project won't fly.

Leadership Rewards Bold.

One of the items I find most useful in asking for a mentor is to let them know that when you are in the position you will reciprocate. And you should. Don't let those words be empty when you've proven yourself. See above reason. You'll be amazed at how these efforts can accelerate your Psycho Success.

CHAPTER FIFTEEN

GPs, LPs, JVs

I would not recommend getting involved in a partnership, because by nature they rarely work. But many times partnerships are necessary; only make sure you have controlling interest. Think GP (General Partner) vs. LP (Limited Partner). The better your friendship or relationship, the worse your partnership will turn out in the end. The horror stories are splattered all over the walls of courthouses across America. One partner blows the company's money leasing a private jet. Another snorts the profits up his nose. Yet another develops an addiction to gambling and strippers. Eventually, one partner realizes he is outperforming the other(s) and someone has to be voted off. Unless you have a controlling interest, it will eventually be you. Don't make that mistake.

Instead, look at the alternative of building several joint ventures. This enables you to do projects on a deal-by-deal basis. You won't be bound by a "partnership agreement" and you won't be bound to each other's personal finances. A joint venture remains alive for a previously agreed upon period of time, so when you outgrow the relationship you simply move on to new joint ventures.

With a partnership, you are married to one person or numerous general partners and sometimes even the LPs. If your partnership spouse lets himself go and becomes fat and lazy, a divorce will be expensive, while a joint venture allows you to have many spouses and much more room to maneuver from both a business and personal perspective.

Realize that there will never be true equality in any business partnership, so protect yourself and your "would-be" partner by setting up joint ventures instead. It will save business relationships and preserve friendships.

CHAPTER SIXTEEN

The Mirror Doesn't Lie

Mr. Superior was holding a companywide meeting. Profits were down so he needed a person to sacrifice to show employees that he was still in full control and still riding herd over all his subordinates. He also needed to ensure he was feared as a leader. During the meeting, Mr. Superior detailed mistakes by this *unnamed* employee before leading up to a big climax where he pointed to Charlie B. Gone and blamed poor Charlie for the failure of the profit sharing plan. And under the bus Charlie went. Two days later, Charlie, in violation of company rule 14(a), brought a firearm to work. Mr. Superior is no longer throwing anyone else under the bus.

Never throw an employee under the bus! You are responsible for that very employee you are crucifying, so when you make statements pointing blame in your company, this ultimately reflects on you. You made the bad hire. You green-lighted the idea. This means the training program you installed sucks. It looks like you have no backbone because you need an excuse and you know how we feel about excuses. You must assume all responsibility for your team or your organization's actions. Have the stones to get out in front of it before anything really does go wrong. And stay away from the sacrificial lamb bullsh*t or someday you'll be that little lamb.

Don't get me wrong; discipline is essential for an organization to continue to perform at a high level. Even though you won't call an employee out in public, in a small team meeting you can talk directly with the employee that spit the bit. This is very effective. Tutor your employees rather than unleashing your ranting-and-raving, hysterical inner beast. Be consistent with this approach through questions about how the company can help him or her make sure another opportunity isn't missed. You will find the communication in that setting very effective.

The peer pressure from other team members will also cause an amazing transformation in the level of performance. It will also keep all the employees consistently maintaining a high effort level for the company. Be the leader whom people can approach. Be one who is fair, whom people can believe in, and you will gain your subordinates' trust, but more importantly their respect too. You are only as good as those that you surround yourself with, because they are a reflection of you. And let's face it, you love you some you.

CHAPTER SEVENTEEN

Guts Have No Chance

In your reception area, there are two people waiting to see you. Both are selling the same product. They are competitors. In the seat closest to the candy dish is a fat, hulking slob. His meaty fingers are tearing into as many Fun Size Snickers bars as fast as he can shove them into his mouth. He slouches as he waits to see you, his gut lapping over his belt. When he stands, the whites of his pockets show because the fabric around his waist is so tight it threatens to rip. When he takes a few steps forward, he breathes hard as his heart labors to meet the overwhelming needs of this gluttonous Jabba the Hut.

Next to him is a tall, lean female. Her hair is neatly done and her clothing is flawless. Instead of hitting the candy dish, she is going over her notes to prepare for the presentation she will shortly give. Suddenly, you appear in the waiting room and see both of them. Who do you think will get the business? Unless the big guy has a price much lower than his hanging gut, he has a less-than-zero chance in closing the deal.

Are either of these two characters you? It's great to work your mind constantly, but it's ridiculous to not get outside and do something physical. This is an edge that many leaders do not take advantage of. To max out your Psycho Success, you must make it a habit every day of doing a physical activity you enjoy. You must experience the outside world. Sure, I understand video games are fun and addicting, but from a business perspective if you are a fat slob, no one will take you seriously. You could be the funniest SOB on the planet, yet behind your back your client is torching you. Why do you think the most successful marketers and account executives make it a point to stay in shape? Because clients don't want to talk to people who eat Krispy Kremes all day. IBM knew this all too well.

IBM would hire recent college graduates, many of them attractive females. IBM would then coach the employees on their products and services. They also had a team of product specialists to back them up if the new hires couldn't answer the more technical questions. IBM knew from numerous studies that there was a much higher success rate of a CIO or top technical director taking the call of a young lady. And once they met her face-to-face, they didn't mind speaking with her again if need be. Who do you want to be: the pizza-stained slouch with shoe inserts or the athletic woman—or man—with the cute smile who gets the business?

CHAPTER EIGHTEEN

Violent Professionals

Each day, you have people who serve your company in various capacities. Look at them as another tool. A surgeon has a nurse to hand him his medical device of choice at the precise time he needs it. Sure he could probably get it himself, but this allows him to focus solely on the procedure. As a result, he is able to perform the surgery more rapidly, increasing the likelihood of success, but also increasing the number of surgeries he can pick up in a day. In a large sense, his nurse can be viewed as a moneymaker.

The two mistakes I see companies make are (1) not realizing the need to hire a professional for seemingly unimportant positions and (2) hiring a professional yet not paying enough to keep them for longer periods of time. Take the surgeon for example. Do you think he wants some half-ass nurse off the street fumbling with his instruments? No, he wants the best and most efficient he can find, because he understands that those extra surgeries he performs add up to huge revenue over the span of just a few years. To max out your Psycho Success, you need to understand the value of hiring the best professionals with the skill set needed to perform at consistently high levels.

> # Cutthroat Pros You Will Always Need: an Attorney, a CPA and a PRS.

Sounds like the beginning of a joke but it's no laughing matter. A lawyer should *save* you money by catching all the mistakes and gotchas in your contracts. Then, he will *make* you money by negotiating the crap out of opposing counsel or an opponent that is not represented. Unless you plan to get a law degree and do the work yourself, hire a quality lawyer who's not a family friend.

Next, the CPA (Certified Public Accountant). Why? Because our form of government is based on income from its citizens, and each year the tax code gets larger. The tax code is now the size of *seven* double-spaced Bibles. A good minister can only quote from one. Imagine Sundays if the Bible were 7x longer in length. The sheer volume of information that must be processed is why you must hire a good, if not great, CPA. These professionals not only save you money by making sure you take every legal deduction you are entitled to through the entities they set up for you, but also by keeping your ass out of hot water if the IRS swears you have violated their code. A top CPA can be a profit center for you and your company through entities and tax shelters that few ever get to take advantage of.

Finally, a PRS (Public Relations Spin Master) professional is vital in today's instant fame and celebrity-driven world. As you may have already discovered, anyone can post anything at anytime about you and your company. A negative post can negatively affect revenue or put you out of business if dirty laundry gets to the wrong clients. I recently traveled to Cancun and wanted to visit a nice restaurant across the street from my hotel. I looked online and the one review that stood out for me was that a rat had been seen in the kitchen enjoying the food. I decided not to go there; however, when I couldn't get in another place I walked over and gave Ratatoullie's a try. I talked to the owner, who said he believed a disgruntled worker had posted about the rat. I could see it was affecting his business.

A great PRS person creates positive press, can spin negative events and manages your reputation. Inoculate your business and take the vaccine *before* you get the virus. PR is a very powerful tool in today's access-to-everything-online world. Don't get caught with your pants down and always promote through this media-savvy professional. The good ones typically have contacts that yield a social power that can produce mad money.

So, now that I have convinced you to hire three key professionals, there are two more points to understand. Hire professionals who are absolutely *cutthroat.* They must be ruthless and highly aggressive. Like General Patton, they must understand the need to *violently execute.*

The second point is trust. You also must trust them. Without trusting their methods, you will accomplish nothing. To find trustworthy, aggressive and cutthroat professionals, you will have to take the time and shop around. What you thought were costs of doing business are actually professionals who will make you Psycho Successful.

CHAPTER NINETEEN

Meritocracy's Rule

Would the Dallas Mavericks have won a World Championship if they selected players based on seniority? Hell no! Successful teams put the players on the floor who give them the best chance of winning. As soon as a player can't cut it anymore, they're gone. Life's tough. Your business should function the same way. Sex, race and age don't matter as long as you can perform at a high level. I have seen businesses hire only young people because they have a ton of energy, yet they couldn't focus on a task and thus couldn't perform at any level, much less a high one. Then there are the businesses that let older employees linger due to seniority instead of phasing them out as their performance drops. Besides being illegal, hiring based solely on age is brainless.

Performing at a high level is all your organization should

worry about, and there must be no doubt in anyone's mind that performance is what is valued in the organization. If you're the manager or CEO, this message needs to be broadcast loud and clear every day to employees through your conversations, actions and promotions. People are paid on performance, nothing else. This also means that there will be a large discrepancy in salaries, bonuses and rewards. That fact will be a part of how the organization is shaped and who is promoted.

> ## Bold Promotes Itself.

As for you, no one should care if you're the biggest asshole on the planet. Your superiors should only care about one thing: are you adding as much value to the organization as possible? This sometimes requires hard decisions, like putting down a once-prized stallion that can no longer stand at stud. If you can't make the hard decisions, hire someone who can, before you become your own worst enemy and put your employees in the bread line. Being a lousy person for doing what's best for the company is not easy, but over time you will grow to like it.

Meritocracies work and they work because everyone

knows how decisions will be made. With you not being harsh or inconsiderate while building a business, people like you will be attracted to this pay-for-performance model.

CHAPTER TWENTY

Audacious Meetings

Meetings serve two purposes: to find solutions and to steer the business in the right direction. An Audacious Meeting may deal with one client or project or it may encompass a larger view. No matter what's being discussed, you must direct the employees to be innovative in their strategic thinking. Teach them to be aggressive and not afraid to speak up. Some of the dumbest ideas have made millions for their creators. Why should your meetings be any different?

Meetings don't just gather for the sake of themselves; the key element to meetings is *people*. And all the people in the meeting must be highly focused. There are two ways to make sure people are focused in meetings, and it all stems from their mindset when they enter the meeting. First, if employees know the meeting starts at a certain time, they should know they had better be in their seats and ready to bring their thunder at stated time. The second aspect is meeting length. Keep your meetings short. If an employee knows the meeting will start at 2:00 and end in fifteen minutes, keeping focused is a no-brainer.

Preparation is another key to a productive meeting. Beforehand, send out an agenda of what will be discussed and decisions that must be me made. This gives each attendee a chance to ponder the itinerary and come up with innovative solutions/ideas for the meeting. It also teaches them to completely think through the idea before they even enter the meeting. If your meeting is a brainstorming session, then *don't* prepare them with an agenda. Do let them know that it's a free-associating session, so they don't fill their brains with twitter trending pop junk and come to the session clouded.

The outcomes of your meeting should not be predetermined; otherwise you could have just sent your commands in an email to all participants. Meetings should be open where a productive dialogue occurs. Ask questions. Questions signal your desire for alternative perspectives, and encourage unique thoughts. Attendees will quickly learn that you are looking for answers, not giving them. But for the love of country, don't allow employees to give lay-up solutions/answers that a four-year-old could have thought of. This is a tremendous waste of time. Audacious Meetings need fresh ideas, bold solutions and solid actionable items that can be taken out of the room. Don't let employees waste time on items that have been put to bed or ideas that would occur to a chimpanzee. If you are getting these kinds of answers and thoughts from your staff, it's time to stop hiring from the short bus and start hiring fearless honey badgers.

Bold Thinks and Operates

on a Far Greater Level.

Audacious Meetings, while on time and short, are informal and loose. Conversations should be unscripted with honest questions and spontaneity. Encourage people to approach and air conflicts. This removes the barriers to fresh innovative ideas and fosters great decision-making. When people express real opinions and are audacious, productivity only increases.

Use whiteboards. I always find whiteboards are great for meetings, as most people need some visualization in order to actually consume and truly learn. PowerPoint slides have their place, but they are never as effective as an expert with a whiteboard when explaining new concepts.

In Audacious Meetings, decisions are made and action

taken. Real results occur that move the needle and propel the company forward. All parties should leave the meeting knowing they are expected to achieve great results given the ideas that come out of Audacious Meetings.

CHAPTER TWENTY-ONE

Numero Uno

Is it ever good to be last? Or Mediocre? Be first in your space/industry. Be the thought leader. Be the innovator. Be the first to disrupt the typical, break the model, run from the standard, breakout with an original thought. And be first to explode the status quo. The first to find *better* has an accelerated climb to dominance. There is a classic line from a recent movie I watched that is so true it is frightening: "To make money in business you have to be first, be smarter or cheat. And we don't cheat."

Look out that window; you are not the only bright guy walking the streets. But being first to *X marks the spot* in the end usually crushes the competition—if it is a well-thought-out, innovative and disruptive idea. You quickly learn that being first is the easiest and best strategy to making money.

Think about the first hyena to a carcass. They typically get their fill with the juiciest parts of the kill and don't have to share what they have already consumed. Think of this situation in terms of your current market or new market.

Bold Is a Contrarian That Perceives Differently and Never Drinks the Kool-Aid.

To illustrate, we took a position in an e-commerce company that had taken off just because of this strategy. The company, Shopforbags.com, was the first true distributor to get their brands of handbags and apparel on the Internet, and they have never looked back. The management team was sharp, but being the first to market on the Internet quickly vaulted the company to sales above $5 million within approximately three years. Before their competitors could even blink, Shopforbags.com had surpassed all of them, and the competitors began to follow suit just to keep up. Only the most well-capitalized competitors still compete with this company that has sold to over 10,000 boutiques and stores across the US.

The point is: there are a lot of smart people in this world with great ideas. The easiest way to Psycho Success is to be first to market.

CHAPTER TWENTY-TWO

Be Frictionless

If you want to have a successful business or brand, make it easy to do business with you. People not only like easy, they *remember* easy. Clients do business with easy. The less friction you have between you and your customers, the more traction you will gain. That is why you should make it your bold mission to remove any issues or barriers from doing business with your company. Your company should be the easiest to do business with in your industry. Use these ideas to streamline your business and watch your profits start to increase almost immediately.

Be flexible. Have an easy-to-remember phone number or email address. Make early morning deliveries. Take credit cards or PayPal. Accept late night pick-ups. Easy payment terms. The point is if you are frictionless, you are memorable. Whatever is holding your customers back from purchasing from you, find a way to remove the roadblock and find a solution. A sharp real estate agent I know got a listing to an expensive vacant house, because she promised the seller weekly photos of the house and that the doors would be checked each day to ensure they were locked. She was being flexible to the needs of her clients. She simply asked a tech-savvy neighborhood kid to check the doors and email her the photos each day. Of course, she paid the kid, and the daily photos greatly impressed the seller. That took about 10 seconds of thought for that simple solution.

The biggest part of being easy to do business with is to be likeable. We are a social society and people hang around other people they find common ground with. That said, find that common ground with potential clients and you stand a much better chance of driving more revenue. You don't have to change an item. Be yourself. Be genuine. Be relaxed. Be funny. Care about your client's business and your likeability will show. Likeability helps develop a strong relationship with your clients and continues to have a lasting impression upon your clients, even if you are not the most inexpensive in the industry. And the relationships, if strong enough, can keep the competition from pilfering your customers.

Another element of being easy to do business with is try to model your business around giving something of value away for free. And I'm not talking about nickel and diming clients to death. Instead, make some part of your services free of charge. Find something of value in your industry, that no one else is giving away free and let your clients know this service is free just for doing business with you. It's a great marketing tool as well. Don't lead with free, but go further with free.

When clients wake up every day and like you, understand it's because you're easy to do business with. Sprinkle in a little free, and you have Psycho Success.

CHAPTER TWENTY-THREE

The Assertive Parent

People make mistakes. So if you want to be successful you have to be forgiving. But that doesn't mean you don't discuss the mistake and emphasize how important it is to correct the mistake. That's where being forceful comes into play. If an employee sh*ts the bed on an account or in an important meeting, they need to know that performing at a high level does not include that mistake. You earn the respect of your employees and clients in many ways by your words and attitude not towards them, but towards the goal at hand and, more specifically, how they are affecting the outcome. As a result, each employee knows what is expected of them and the level of production they must achieve.

Many times clients are the same way. There is a very good reason why a client comes to a professional who has a reputation of sustained success. Deep down they want to be told what to do about their specific need or predicament. Clients love the brutal honesty and the candid remarks about their issues as long as you bring well-thought-out solutions to the table. If they just wanted affirmation about what they should do, they would have hired another "yes man" consultant or their old strung-out high school buddy. Here's the key: clients understand you aren't their parents and, as long as you don't tell them that directly, they want you to be confident and forceful in asserting your professional opinion. But bring the results or you just become annoying. Clients and employees alike respect this attitude and understand the difference between accommodating vs. being an a-hole.

CHAPTER TWENTY-FOUR

Knuckleheads and Startups

Every business you elicit commerce from was a startup at one point. Your business was a startup and may still be. Do you feel people should not do business with you because of perceived handicaps?

Startup companies are what make this country great, but it is not lost on me that some of these founders that start these companies talk a great game, but are knuckleheads when it comes to actually doing business. Take advantage of these situations.

Many times these newly-formed companies want to make a splash in the industry and will offer very attractive prices to do business with their organizations. Sometimes they give their services or products away free for a period of time. Don't be scared. Step up and test them, but with forethought.

Obviously for most startups, capital or cash flow—or the lack thereof—can be problematic. If a startup is going to supply your business with goods, make sure both parties understand the payment terms so neither company gets hurt. If you are thinking of supplying your goods or services to a startup customer, make sure you understand their financial situation and know it is not uncommon to ask for their financial statements or a signed personal guarantee from the founders. Limit your downside risk when doing business with startups, but don't forego the price breaks because of their perceived lack of funds. A little due diligence will help you make the decision. Hell, consider taking a credit card from your startup customers and make it effortless on everyone. It's just another way of making it easy to do business with your firm, but it goes without saying: it's good to have a relationship with a backup supplier or suppliers.

Startups carry a certain risk, but some careful investigation, forethought and enormous price breaks, sometimes through efficiencies, make doing business with startups a path to Psycho Success.

CHAPTER TWENTY-FIVE

Be Everywhere

Marketing. Marketing. Marketing. You need to be everywhere. This is vital to any business that wishes to *remain* in business. I look at marketing as tossing chum in the water. Sure you could pilot your boat around the ocean for days with a pork butt on the end of a big hook, and you may eventually catch a shark. But think how much more effective it is to spread chum over a small area and have your pick of the numerous sharks. That's what explosive marketing does for you.

> **Bold Gets Noticed and Bold Sells Bold.**

Today the marketing choices are endless, yet so is the potential for spending a lot of money on unproven channels. Being everywhere doesn't mean blowing your yearly advertising budget in one week. You must be smart with where you advertise, but don't be afraid of marketing on the edge and advertising in new channels. Many times early adopters can see immediate results if they understand the platform and the channel. And the only way to do this is to experience that customer stream. Use cutting edge techniques and don't fear stepping outside of your norm if only for testing purposes. Technology can quickly clear the clutter of what is working and where your ROI is slim to none.

Social media is everywhere and always comes to mind in marketing products, as many people feel it is the future. But channels need to be quantified. Social media is not free because it takes time and labor, but it can be very cost effective to reach hundreds of customers with just a few clicks of a mouse. If you don't understand today's technology, hire someone who does. Consider Twitter, Facebook, Pinterest, LinkedIn or industry-served networks to communicate with your clients and suppliers just as you did when there was only email.

Take Twitter for instance. The platform is an excellent tool for marketing when done correctly. If a person understands how to increase followers and still get your brand's message out to the world, they can become very valuable. Many PR firms have departments that handle these types of social media activities. We see the channel as a living newsletter that gives insights to your customers on numerous topics in your industry. If you have new products, again let everyone know about them, but recognize that Twitter must also include news and notes that don't tie in directly to your business. Have fun with it. If your clients have some interesting stories you could share via Twitter, re-tweet them and make them feel appreciated if it is relevant to your industry. A big key here is to make sure you use hash tags properly and the followers will begin to multiply.

Finally, set up your advertising so that you track the revenue from the various advertising channels. With today's technology, tracking the different advertising channels through known analytics is easier than ever. We periodically track to known metrics in our industry and have found this to be a very good way of understanding how our ROI stacks up against our competition. Cost per lead and revenue per lead. These two metrics don't always give you the same answer, because you may produce a ton of leads that are worthless, while another form of advertising produces a few leads that are homeruns each time. You can market, market, market, but without quantitative analysis you are wasting valuable dollars. Chum the waters and then choose the best marketing channels for your business.

CHAPTER TWENTY-SIX

The Reality of Perception

Society truly wants to believe everything they read, see or hear. Thousands of people will read what is on the Internet or in a friend's email and go on blind faith that it must be true, even though the image was obviously Photoshopped to illustrate a point. A friend I know was scared to flash her car's high beams during the day, because she read that gang members single you out and track you down as part of some insane initiation ritual. It's a myth, but the perception is that it's reality because it's been reinforced time and time again. Hence, the myth becomes reality.

Make sure you are wary of acts of blatant persuasion through the use of biased Internet resources as a basis for argument's sake, but also be cognizant of the fact that the Internet can be used to your advantage in business and negotiation. The fact that you aren't the largest brand on the block or the 800-pound gorilla in your industry doesn't mean you can't act like it. I dealt with a business that had an office in a high-rise in downtown New York City. Their website showed a black-and-white photo of this building and talked about their business in terms of global reach. Later I discovered their business was nothing more than a single guy who had set up a lockbox in the building. As part of his lease he was allowed to use the photo in advertising. He actually worked out of his home in New Jersey, but on the Internet he looked like Mr. Universe. You see where I'm going with this?

On the flip side, I have seen huge companies resemble little more than a ripe pimple on the Internet. Why do they do this? The likely reason is that their massive size has caused them to not care or misunderstand the changing digital world. These companies miss the fact that Joe Lunchbox is sometimes naive and doesn't know all this when he goes on the Internet. When he decides whom he will call for said services, the firm in the New York City office building with the lockbox gets the call instead of the lazy, large, archaic firm with their ill-conceived web presence.

On websites or brochures, use facts and figures to your advantage. These can always be skewed one way or another. For example: *98% of people with a higher education who read this chapter understand the message.* Sounds good, right? Other great tools I see small firms use are press releases. Consistently fresh material on the Internet and great search engine optimization website features assure potential customers that you are a relevant player with phenomenal products and services in your industry. And don't overlook good reviews from customers. Encourage your customers to evaluate your firm, even if you have to add incentives. These make your website more relevant and easier to find during a search on the Internet.

> ## Bold Understands Reality
> ## But Deals in Perception.

The cold hard fact is that most people are reluctant to do business with smaller, unproven companies, but with the perception of a larger business, your potential customers will never know the difference. Reality becomes perception and the *"fake it till you make it"* mantra certainly is much easier to pull off in the digital age. Take advantage of this fact and grow your business.

CHAPTER TWENTY-SEVEN

Never Apologize

Never apologize for making a profit. That is your primary goal as a business owner. Nowadays, people act like profit is a dirty word. Unintelligent people protest if someone is making too much profit. I never understood this argument. Where do these people want to live? Oppressed China? All you have to do is remove profit and see what happens. In the late 1970s, President Carter began regulating oil prices, which stopped imports, and magically no gas appeared at the pumps. When government sets the price below a profitable level, work stops. It was a simple lesson: take the profit out of something and the product disappears.

In Communist Russia in the 1970s, the government thought it would be much more efficient to have one big toilet paper factory than several different factories competing against each other. Since profit was a dirty word in Russia, they set up one huge factory cranking out toilet paper for all of the country. Of course, with no competition and no incentive to make a profit, corruption was rampant. Quality dropped. Supplies plummeted. The supple, soft toilet paper quickly turned into something just this side of sandpaper. What were they going to do, buy from someone else? Fortunately, politicians and the elite were able to get a softer version out the backdoor for a few *rubles on the palms,* while the cries from the peasants about their sore asses fell upon deaf ears. Russia wiped away the profit from the toilet paper industry, leaving the average Russian with no choice. For years it was hard for the Russian people to sit comfortably.

Everything flows from the goal of making a profit. For example, taking care of the customer is *not* the highest priority. Yep, you heard me correctly.

> **Making a Profit Is Your Highest Priority.**

Making a profit is the highest priority, because any business will learn that pissing off a customer is bad for revenue, unless that customer is continually asking for more, but unwilling to pay for it. For those, "Let me introduce you to my competition. They really want to work with you!"

Quality is another example. Quality is not job one. If a company makes top quality products but doesn't turn a profit, the company can quickly go insolvent. We call these bankrupt entities, donors of cheap assets. There is a happy medium, but no profits means no cash to reinvest, which means failure.

Making a profit shouldn't be the only goal. However, any business must strive to make *as much profit as humanly possible.* Profit is the single, most accurate, all-encompassing measure of whether your company is truly the best at what it does. When profits slow, everyone in the supply chain suffers. Maximizing the bottom line is how you motivate employees who will soon realize the profits/value they bring to the company is commensurate with their performance, and that motivates everyone. Never apologize for your success. You've earned it.

CHAPTER TWENTY-EIGHT

30 for 30

Employment laws don't allow discrimination based on age. However, when I walk into many businesses, I see age discrimination. In one business, I saw that almost all employees were over the age of forty. Why is this? Many employers have tried young employees because they work cheaper than older, more seasoned professionals. Then they discover that many young people have a tough time concentrating, or they have relationship issues that cloud their thoughts. Or they stay up late and kick back a good amount of drinks with friends, and they display far less loyalty. These traits are really about just being young, but the traits can result in grave problems for employers. Eventually, the owners of the business grow older, and so does their workforce as the younger workers weed themselves out. Ultimately, in many instances young people are relegated to the retail and restaurant industries where their warm bodies are more important than their possibly new innovative and fresh ideas.

When it comes to a staff, you need to have the 30/30 rule: 30% of your staff must be under the age of 30. Why? Because young people bring a different dynamic to the table, and their fresh ideas are those of the new generations. They typically understand how today's fast-moving society and impulsive, instant-gratification-seeking clients think. They may not have the years of expertise your senior employees do, but they can certainly see the forest for the trees.

Fresh Ideas Are Some of the Boldest Ideas.

Technology and social media are two critical tools that come natural to young people, giving them a 40,000-foot view over a variety of topics. And 40,000-foot views are mandatory for Psycho Success in business. Even Ray Kroc, the founder of McDonald's, used technology of the day to get a higher view in a helicopter to observe traffic patterns when deciding where to locate his next restaurant. Employees under 30 don't do this physically, but they do it theoretically, because they grew up with much different perspectives and live life in a way that generations before never have. Listen to them. They could hold the creative key that clients are looking for and push your business into the Psycho stratosphere.

CHAPTER TWENTY-NINE

Embrace the Chaos

To most, social media is a luxury. But it is being woven into the fabric of businesses tighter and tighter each day. I know tweeting and Facebooking customers can be a beating and add expense to your business, but don't avoid social media. Embrace it. The sooner you do, the faster sales will increase as you learn the tips and tricks to acquiring more fans and followers that help your message reach more of your market.

Understand social media is such a large piece of the mobile space that is growing at such an accelerated pace engineers cannot keep up with demand. A large part of this push is due to businesses being created around social media and mobile applications (Apps). There are hundreds of websites that can honestly say 20% of their business comes from their efforts on social media. Mobile devices and social media will continue to grow your sales. Don't be the guy who doesn't understand the social shifts and continues to carry an irrelevant flip phone. Throw it away and embrace the new paradigm of the social media channel.

Bold Understands Everyone Is an Influencer.

Every business will have customer issues. These unhappy customers typically will take to the Internet and especially to social media to voice their complaints and how much your company sucks. Don't hide from them. Meet them head on. Acknowledge their issue and publicly take steps to resolve it. Social media is forcing companies to be more transparent with consumer issues. The more you hide issues, the more they gain relevance online. The longer the issues linger, the more people come to know about them.

Finally, when using social media it's okay to market to your fans and followers, but not all the time. Only 20% of what you say on social media should be self-promotional. Provide some non-self-serving content. Understand that clients, customers and the general public desire unique thoughts and a deeper connection to your brand. This can be accomplished through games, quizzes, questions, surveys and industry articles. But the key is to make the conversations humorous, enjoyable and relevant to your social media feed. With 20% of your content devoted to self-promotion, the other 80% should show what a great kick-ass brand you are and the connection to your customers. Get busy in social media. Embrace the online chaos and be even more relevant to your industry.

CHAPTER THIRTY

More Effective Than Waterboarding

When negotiating the sale of *anything* don't toss your marbles and become the insane, babbling salesperson who is only recreating an infomercial of what the client could have taken from the brochure. This behavior is far too common for many salespeople. Don't be common, be different. These jabbering salespeople think the client is going to walk unless everything is on the table. Slow down, Turbo, and take time to find common ground. Get the client to like you by amazing them with a dazzling personality or a much more innovative approach to your sales technique. More importantly, get the clients talking about their businesses, their likes, their vision, their uniqueness in their market and why they took your meeting. Through casual conversation with no intent to rush a sales pitch, a routine sales meeting can easily be turned into a partner or investor meeting with both parties being open about their business commonalities.

Ask to add your client to your newsletter as this makes them a team member instead of just a client. Ask opened-ended questions. "Can you tell me about your unique vision for the next year?" Or "Can you tell me how this specific business unit functions?" If you ask yes or no questions they won't be revealing much, and it soon becomes an examination. Act relaxed with a conversational tone and stay away from the fact-finding, waterboarding, interrogational attitude and questioning.

But better than those techniques is the power of scarcity. There is something to be said about scarcity when dealing with clients. Don't always pick up the phone when your client calls. Clients want to know you are in demand and that you are relevant in their industry. Not being at the client's beck and call accomplishes this. Subconsciously they will begin to believe, "That guy has to have something special. He's always busy." Note: don't forget to return the calls later in the day.

In crunch-time situations, the telling-not-selling technique typically works with the right client's personality. When clients are looking for quick, situational expertise, great salesmen don't need to ask too many questions, because they quickly transition into "here's what you need to do..." If what you say is from a different perspective and offers a solution the client's team couldn't have thought of, you have just landed a client for life.

Also, many times through the ease of conversation you will find your product is not a fit for what they want. Don't be afraid to recommend someone else. If you try to push the square peg through the round sales funnel, eventually the client will figure out you're not a fit. Get out in front of this embarrassment and this contact will produce far more introductions than actual clients. Why? They will feel like they owe you a favor. When the client is the priority, your sales techniques can take many shapes. You'll be surprised at the success and effectiveness of these techniques when used properly.

CHAPTER THIRTY-ONE

Analytics, Analytics, Analytics!

Seek, search, find and use the most up-to-date analytical tools for your business. Typically these powerful tools are used with regard to websites, providing data about specific customer demographic trends, analysis of merchandise purchased and why the correlation between the two. Almost any kind of business can use analytical tools to understand their clients better. It's a glorified super computer that gives great insight into why your customers chose to purchase or do business with you. The more you know about your customers and what motivates them, their wants, their desires or simply what brought them to your business, the easier and more cost effective it is to market to them. These factors help companies increasingly develop efficiency and scale at much higher rates than before.

The latest analytical tools will consider customer demographics, geography, shopping habits, education, purchase price, time of day, social network influences, online behavior and many other factors. We really do live within the Matrix, and Big Brother is always watching. Everyone can know everything about everyone, and information is power. Your end game for all of this is to find your net promoter score, meaning: how likely a customer is to recommend your business/product to a friend without being prompted. Once you find this out you can then go out and do more targeted promoting.

Analytical tools will also help you better understand your competition and where they are successful. It's surprising what information can be gleaned from specific Google searches, press releases, newsletters, public emails, advertisements and public filings from publicly held corporations. We often massage data sources such as these to discover new markets that we are not actively pursuing but know an opportunity exists. Analytics come in many shapes and forms, but a good enterprise software program can be found for the budget conscious, or many of these applications can be found on the Internet for free. Ask your marketing guru. He can steer you towards numerous online resources as well.

> # Psycho Companies Are Internet-savvy and Lean on Analytics.

Remember, unless it's free, if you can't measure your individual marketing activities, then why do them at all? You're wasting valuable time and marketing dollars on blind faith, betting that everyone is a customer for your business. Bullsh*t. Find your avatar (customer profile most likely to purchase your product/service) and target your marketing to these avatars through the use of analytics.

Even the most edgy marketing tools or techniques should be able to measure the effectiveness of a marketing campaign applying analytical strategies. These applications will always be able to better your company's ROI, no matter the marketing activity. Be the first to use these tools in your industry, and you'll reach efficiency before most do, keeping your competitors wondering how you continue to increase your customer base, revenue and profits while they're sucking wind stuck with the same old ways of shotgun marketing.

CHAPTER THIRTY-TWO

Forecasting Flexibility

Forecasting is the bane of a salesman's existence. No business ever made a penny from a forecast. Psycho Success is about marketing for increased revenue and for optimizing profits, not forecasting. Sitting down and mapping out a forecast takes time away from actual sales, phone time, calling new clients and time upselling current clients. Look, I understand why they are done and they *do* have a place in the process, but at most once a quarter.

I often see confusion among sales managers regarding sales goals and forecasts. You can ask a salesperson: "How many units will you sell this week?"

The salesperson will give the answer that represents their *goal.* "I think I can sell fifty units." It took less than thirty seconds for the salesperson to give that answer, yet the manager believes he just got the *forecast* for that week. If it were an actual forecast, the salesperson would have had to examine economic trends, their clients' budget policies, their competitors' strategies and hundreds of other factors to deliver an intelligent answer, not to mention always begging the customer for what they think they might purchase that week or month. That kind of chore would take *hours*. And that assumes the salesperson even *possesses* that type of ability. As for the sales manager, he or she was likely promoted from the sales group and may not have that knowledge or skill either. Time is of the essence. Do you even want them to take the time to develop that skill?

Most managers have too much data. Great companies have analytical tools at their fingertips but still maintain a sense of being instinctual. These great companies make the correct decisions with limited data analysis, and do so at lightning fast speeds. They don't wait on every available—often trivial—piece of information on a deal. Not only are they intuitive and fast, they are extremely flexible. They have spent their time wisely, analyzing deals and talking to the players and are able to pivot when models and deals break down. Instead of spending hours and days trying to nail a 50% accurate forecast, they have readied their company to pivot with whatever they deem necessary to get a deal done. Flexibility, not forecasting, is their main priority. Put down the forecast spreadsheet and contact a prospect instead.

CHAPTER THIRTY-THREE

Customer Satisfaction Can Lead to Insolvency

What? This goes against everything that you have read or learned. How can customer satisfaction lead to insolvency? Think of it this way: I spent the day hiking down through the Grand Canyon. It was hot. I was tired and I needed a cold beverage to recharge. A small shack near the campground had some supplies. I went in and saw my favorite Vitamin Water chilling in ice. Normally the water costs $1.50 and sometimes goes on sale for 99¢. When I asked how much, the clerk said, "$5.45." My first thought was, "Are you F'n crazy!" I was not happy, but I dug into my pocket and produced the money. It was only later that I asked myself, "How did they get those supplies to such a remote place? Where does the ice come from? Is there even electricity to make ice?"

I'm sure the business owner understood that I would not

be happy. Hell, he's probably heard much harsher terms used to describe his prices, yet he charged it anyway because he knew he had to maintain margins and make a profit in order to remain in business. Making a profit was their number one goal, not satisfying me. Although you can bet I was satisfied when that icy, delicious Vitamin Water began pouring down the back of my throat. In fact, the more I thought about it, the more I decided I would have gladly ponied up $10 for a bottle. Money does buy some happiness.

Striking the right balance between what your clients are willing to pay for your products or services is always a slippery slope, but this grey area is where the profits lie. And in today's environment it's winner take all. To do this, your company must provide elements of differentiation, just like the business owner selling the Vitamin Water: they were right where I needed them, when I needed them and with no other competitor in sight. These elements of scarcity and isolation in the market translated into Psycho Success for the business owner, not how satisfied I was as a customer. The majority of customers recognizes and perceives that to get a good product on their terms, they must pay a little more. They know it. You know it. So don't let your customer satisfaction surveys cloud your head with mindless pricing. Protect your margins and market like hell.

CHAPTER THIRTY-FOUR

Know Your Exits

Have you ever been stuck in an investment not knowing when you might see your money again through no fault of your own? It sucks. Every investment, business or project has a starting point where your time, money, creativity and genius begin. Make sure *before* you apply all these significant resources that you know how you are pulling your investment out the deal or if the business were to go in an unintended direction. Much of this comes with experience and a good attorney or mentor. To know how you are getting out of the investment before you get in is about knowing the market or space in which you are deploying resources. This strategy also leaves you flexible in case a better opportunity walks by.

I remember reading about the harbor in Singapore back in the 1800s, where the captains would let off their men for shore leave. Thirty percent would not return because they were just having too much fun or passed out or found something else to occupy their time. Missing that many men made it almost impossible to set sail on another voyage. The captains had sailed into this port, but failed to understand their exit strategy when it came to human capital. However, all was not lost. These captains worked in concert with the local bars and brothels to establish "special" happy hours. The businesses would advertise free booze and girls to attract the sailors. Once inside, the ship captains would wait, and when the men had a few too many and passed out, they would be taken back aboard. A very unconventional exit strategy to ensure the continuity of their business, but an exit strategy nevertheless. Unfortunately for the sailors, they had left the ship without a proper exit strategy.

> **Know Your Exit *Before* Taking on a Project.**

Understand how you are getting your capital out before advancing to a cash position from which you can no longer pull your equity out. If you don't know, ask. In today's economy, it is very important to be agile, to be nimble and to take advantage of opportunities as they arise. To be first is to win the opportunity and reap the rewards, and to do this you must keep your balance sheet liquid. But first always know your exits.

CHAPTER THIRTY-FIVE

Complexity Decreases Capacity

As a business becomes more and more complex, it becomes more difficult to extract the different expenses as more layers are added. If you aren't sure where your company is making money—or losing it—follow the steps below to simplify your way to Psycho Success:

1. Analyze your profitability by each market. There are often large profit disparities among lines of business, brands, products and customers. Knowing exactly *where* you're making money and *how* is the first step to making more of it. I worked with one business and discovered they were selling the crap out of Product A, while Product B gathered dust. Then I looked at the profitability of each product. Product B made three times as much profit as Product A, yet the sales staff found it easier to sell Product A to customers because the paperwork was

cleaner and the commissions were better. Once I straightened out the semantics of selling each product, Product B quickly outsold Product A and crushed it for the company, making the company 2x more profitable.

2. Make sure each brand and SKU is pulling its weight. Most sizable companies today have numerous brands or individual items called SKUs (stock-keeping units) that contribute little to the bottom line. By targeting profitable ones and cutting the rest loose, you can free up significant capacity and resources in several departments with negligible loss in revenue and volume. The biggest plus is that you aren't holding large amounts of inventory on your books, which only ties up more cash. If you just have to carry some of these bottom-feeder, low-volume items, consider a strategic partnership with your supplier and let them stock the inventory while you only take a commission by selling it through your marketing channels.

Take some time to discover which pipes are bringing in the most profit to your company, and then make those pipes bigger.

CHAPTER THIRTY-SIX

Passion Never Works

Passionate employees beat talent, when talent doesn't work hard. People are more creative when they feel passionate about their work. Whether they are driven by interest, enjoyment, satisfaction or personal challenge, they are more likely to take risks, look for multiple solutions to issues and seek out the best solution rather than the easiest. Are these not the people you want working for you?

> **Bold Likes the Heavy Lifting and**
> **Takes up the Slack When Others Won't.**

Get to know potential hires as thoroughly as possible *before* you have a position for them specifically. Ask them why they chose their specific skills to enhance, what drives them, what their passions are, what disappointments they've had and what a dream job would look like. Look for energy and desire in their eyes as they talk about the work itself, and then listen for a deep hunger to do something unforeseen and the willingness to execute on it. When you talk to their references, listen for mentions of passion and execution.

Yet finding and hiring this kind of employee requires effort. Of course, you want to know all you can, because the more you know about a potential employee, the higher probability of making your team a better one. I like to first talk to a candidate on the phone and go over their portfolio of work I see on Linkedin. If I see promise, I'll have them come in for a brief interview. If I'm still impressed, I will do some digging online, ask them to do a project (covered in this book) and call all their references and common contacts we share. Finally, I'll call them in for one last interview to go over anything I may have found in my research. After three contacts with the potential hire, I should still see that passion and excitement. If I don't, then it was all a show to get the position and there may be no real passion behind what they do. Find passionate people and they will be a great long-term asset. Missing on an employee happens, but don't let it happen too much, or you may be the missing employee.

CHAPTER THIRTY-SEVEN

Inspire by Proxy

Let's face it, we all want to be heard and respected, but at our essence, all we really want is to be liked by the people close to us, and many times people we just met. We all want to be *the most interesting man in the world*. To many of us it comes naturally, but for the majority of society, we must work on these personable skills. Yet no amount of practice or standing in the mirror will turn you into Winston Churchill, Ronald Reagan, Steve Jobs or even George Bush. But there are ways to increase your charisma and win over more people and your team by changing how you communicate.

> Passion + Hard Work Beats Talent,
>
> When Talent Doesn't Work Hard.

People love the excitement of getting behind a leader who is all in, passionate and determined to conquer the market in which your business resides. To take a project or idea of the business and express your sincere conviction in the right context will create a perception of increased charisma. This will reveal the quality of your character, which establishes your credibility with your team and/or listeners. They will then identify and align themselves with you and the goals you have for your business. Demonstrate authority by setting high goals and conveying confidence that you and your team can achieve extraordinary results. People naturally want to follow a confident, bold and strong leader. As their leader, inspire your team daily as you believe in what you say and what you do has real meaning. Let that flag fly. If you are confident your team can reach their goals, your team will be confident in you as a leader, hence increased charisma by proxy.

CHAPTER THIRTY-EIGHT

Hidden Gems

To succeed in business today you need to know what your customers truly want. Is it price, better customer service, shorter delivery times? Companies routinely use all kinds of analyses, like focus groups, customer panels and other methods to obtain this info. All are good methods and have their place, but just as traditional research has its limits, there is a better way. To get a more focused view for far less expense, go to your frontline employees. They often get an unfiltered view of how customers interact with your product, service or business. Ask your receptionist which customers seem in a good mood coming in and especially leaving after a visit. Sales floor personnel are gems. They know where customers go first and their attitudes towards almost every product. They are a reflection of your customer. Don't overlook those who are actively interacting and engaging with the customer. The closer to your customer you can get, the better the profits will be.

Of course, there is one more way that works all the time: ask your customers. If you can locate several of your customers, ones able to express themselves who aren't hindered by worrying about hurting your fragile feelings, you will obtain loads of customer feedback. Many times these customers will point out not only issues they don't like about your business or products and want changed, but why they love doing business with you. While these particularly well-spoken customers may not always be representative of your company, the feedback they provide can be huge. However you get the information, make sure you use it.

CHAPTER THIRTY-NINE

Adaptive Babysitting

When you manage a team of people, constantly adapt your leadership style to meet the team's needs and specialties. There are four types of approach to leadership: direct, coaching, supporting and delegating. Depending on the level of your employee's competence, skills and commitment, in order to achieve the most productivity, you must choose which works best for your team.

1. **Direct Leadership** - When your employees are learning new skills, be clear and direct on what these skills will do for the business and the individual personally over the long term. Make sure tasks are clearly defined and monitor the team's progress to make sure they're not faltering on reaching their goals.

2. **Coaching Leadership** - Periodic coaching is needed

when your employee is learning new skills, but must be balanced with the freedom to make mistakes and learn from them.

3. Supporting Leadership - Be supportive and encouraging of highly competent employees who lack confidence. Giving them confidence is the game-changer for these types of people.

4. Delegating Leadership - With employees who are both exceptionally motivated and experienced, delegate tasks. They already know how to get it done. These employees are fire-and-forget, profit-making missiles.

Your leadership responsibility is to locate the sweet spot between handholding and empowering. Too much handholding, and you will have a team that is powerless to do anything unless you supervise each step. If empowering is done correctly, after six months of training you will find your team and its individuals where you'd like to see them: confident, capable and productive. At that point, you will have professional employees who know they have the freedom to do their jobs their way, and as long as high level results are attained, they will be able to do what they have been trained and coached to do without full-time supervision.

CHAPTER FORTY

Endangering the Prairie Dog

Team collaboration now occurs all the time in personal cubicles, in hallways or virtually through technology. It is now more often spontaneous and informal and not typically planned in advance. Unfortunately, most current work environments are still dominated by offices or cubicles that slow employees down by not only their configuration, but by their thoughtless barriers to conversation, rarely matching the new collaborative reality we need in business today.

> **Prairie Dogging:**
>
> **The Simultaneous Pop-up of Several Heads**
>
> **When Something Interesting**
>
> **Is Happening Around the Cubicles.**

Most work environments provide little choice regarding where and how one must work. Individual cubicles separate people from one another. Buildings are oftentimes sectioned off by departments with different access codes, with collaborative and cooperation spaces having to be reserved well in advance. Areas with audio and video for global collaboration and teleconferencing are extremely limited in most workplaces. Even social spaces usually lack power sources or Internet access. Team collaboration is challenging enough without the above barriers of underperforming workspaces. Solve these issues with the following:

1. Location diversity - Your business must have areas for individual work, hallways for easy social exchange, rooms equipped with A/V technology and tools for collaborative work. These types of spaces allow people to choose freely: "Where is the best space for me to finish my project?" The days of the unapproachable office are history. Hell, we always consider taking meetings offsite, because it stimulates creativity for the project.

2. Four to six people work best - When it comes to collaboration, the best spaces easily accommodate four to six people. If the meeting is any larger than four to six people, most employees will feel pressure to not speak out and be heard due to embarrassment or the feeling of being overwhelmed by stronger personalities. Optimal collaborative spaces for four to six people typically produce results, and we live for results.

3. **Provide essential social tools** - Effective team collaboration involves knowledge exchange, white-boarding, brainstorming, the inclusion of different perspectives and hundreds of A and B testing scenarios. Provide whiteboards that allow employees to see the ideas and create visual connections. You want more effective employees; give them the collaborative tools to make this happen. Take action, and decisions will happen at a higher rate of speed.

4. **Specific dedicated teams need their own spaces** - These are spaces where teams can hold onto ideas, samples, visuals and conversations that have long passed. Giving them the opportunity to revisit those notes and conversations at a later time is huge. Maintaining a "one project" mindset for all employees involved sharpens focus and produces great expedited results. Is there anything better than quicker decisions that lead to higher profitability?

Providing a first-class environment for your employees to produce brilliant solutions is the best way to achieve Psycho Success.

CHAPTER FORTY-ONE

The Profitability of Credibility

One of the most critical traits of an effective business leader is credibility. It's much like knowing Agent 007 is going to effectively and efficiently find a way to finish the job. James Bond flat out does *it* Hollywood style. If you don't have *it*, you must find *it* and bring *it*. Your company/team must believe in you and your ability to execute your own strategy. If they don't, you'll struggle to motivate anyone who works for you or with you.

Never assume your credibility is apparent just by showing up. You are no different. You must demonstrate your credibility by showing your willingness to get down in the trenches and get dirty. You must "out exert" and "out imagine" your competition 24/7. Do not fail in always keeping your promises, meeting deadlines and generally modeling the behavior you're trying to encourage in your team and in your business. This means always being prepared for collaborative sessions, presentations and meetings.

You must hold others accountable just as you would hold yourself accountable. Treat employees fairly and be consistent. As credibility begins to mature and bear fruit with your employees, you must not only use your power and influence for the benefit of others, but also to exert your vision for the business. This visualization should include that you expect everyone to focus on profitability and always be thinking considerably bigger as the World Is Not Enough. Remember that once you've established your credibility, it's extremely important to continue to demonstrate how trustworthy you are going forward. People want to take pride in their work, and especially in their leader, and that starts with you. Hold yourself accountable. Make your team proud and the execution of your vision will lead to increased profits.

CHAPTER FORTY-TWO

Taxing Yourself to Revenue

I hate to say it, but government taxation is a necessary evil that is essential to your business. Paying your taxes is now thought of as one of the most heinous acts a person must do in their life, but you can use this hostility to your company's advantage.

We all know the taxation system has been broken for quite some time. Many have lost faith in all tiers of government with its bureaucratic nonsense, unrealistic timelines and finger pointing. To a large extent, we can all agree that the government and its taxation policies have far outgrown what our founding fathers intended. The paperwork alone will bury a small business. I certainly don't know a person who isn't angry with both political parties for almost never striking a balance in Washington. And the divide only seems to grow worse each year. Clearly there is a strong dislike in the general population of paying taxes, even though we all know it is necessary. The thought that we are paying our hard earned income into a bureaucratic system with antiquated tax policies is flat out maddening.

Use this to your business' advantage when marketing to your customers. Play the government taxation against your customer through marketing. Most people demonstrate the phenomenon of tax aversion and attempt to avoid paying taxes at all costs. So let's use this as a psyche to increase revenue. Did you know research shows people have a stronger preference to escape tax-related costs than to avoid equal size (or larger) costs unrelated to taxes? Texas, for example, has a sales tax holiday each August when parents are shopping for back-to-school clothes. Texas consumers will spend a large amount of money buying clothes to save a mere 8.5% rather than save 20% at the sale that occurred right before the tax holiday. There's something about sticking it to Uncle Sam that makes people spend money.

Think about it, tax aversion affects consumer preferences in numerous areas such as: in-store purchases, financial investment and job selection. Hell, something could be said that only a few years ago tax aversion played a large role in why the Internet initially became popular. Not only was it much more convenient and easier for commerce, it was tax-free. As the country becomes more and more fed up with government, this aversion will almost certainly grow stronger as well.

Use this consumer behavior in your marketing and ease off the sales and discounts in order to attract customers. Instead, offer "Tax-Free". It could be for a day, applied to a particular item, bundled orders, etc. Strong research shows that customers would prefer to go tax-free and save only 8% vs. saving 15% on a discounted sale, solely due to the nature of what the word *tax* relates to in the American psyche. You can't use tax-free all the time, but when you do it's a powerful weapon for driving consumers to your business.

CHAPTER FORTY-THREE

Resumes Are Toast

Resumes are dead. Interviews are for presentation. Linkedin is useful. References are overrated. Portfolios are something a person may or may have not done. Test-driving is now the answer.

I believe projects or assignments are the future of hiring, especially professional hiring. If you want to be a serious firm, you will ask serious candidates to do a series of assignments to even sniff a job offer. Talented potential employees will engage in real-world assignments, testing their abilities to deliver actual value on their own.

This is why so many times social capital is used in bringing on new team members. Friends or acquaintances know you, but also know what you can do and if you have the ability to help the company. You get the position, not just through networking, but by people realizing your value through accomplishments and somewhat following your career by mutual relationships.

Projects Are the New Job Interviews.

Businesses have learned the hard way that no amount of interviewing, reference checking or psychological testing is a substitute for actually working with a candidate on a real project. Too many times candidates have styled, blow-dried and hair-sprayed their previous jobs and accomplishments to get a position they can't handle or aren't fit for. When the first unfortunate breeze blows, an employer often discovers they only hired a bad comb-over. Once they spit the hair from their mouth, the firm doles out a severance package, unemployment benefits and other assorted crap for yet another hiring mistake.

Throw out the "Tell me a little about yourself" interview question. The real question will be: Can you rise to the challenge and help redesign a social media campaign, document a tricky bit of software, edit a keynote presentation, produce a webinar or review a CAD layout for a Chinese partner?

Exploitive? Maybe, but it cuts your overall hiring costs, and you will have a much better understanding of what talents your candidate is truly bringing to your team or business. If they were a major league player years ago, but are now in double A, you will find that out. If they never were a major league player, that will quickly become apparent.

Typically, candidates must sign NDAs (Non-Disclosure Agreements). And yes, these tasks effectively pit candidates against each other. But there's nothing fake or artificial about the value they're expected to offer the team. Organizations must treat hiring as part of their on-boarding process. Hiring becomes more holistic rather than just warm bodies with great resumes. More importantly, everyone in the enterprise now "gets" that people are only hired if—*and only if*—they deliver something above and beyond a decent paper trail.

On the surface, it may appear that the main reason why "projects are the new job interviews" is because it is more efficient and a more effective mechanism to gain a true measure of a candidate. Yet the true reason is that most talented people typically like having real-world opportunities to shine and succeed. If they have talent, confidence and ability, it will show. Then you can add a valuable member to your team, instead of some worthless bag of hot air sporting a comb-over.

CHAPTER FORTY-FOUR

The Stack Rank Bounce

From your sales staff to warehouse workers, a great way to improve overall performance and add revenue to the bottom line is to inform employees where they stack rank against other employees by metrics that pertain to their position. Once management commits to this, a decision must be made to publicly disclose it or privately inform the employees. Public disclosure can quickly motivate most employees, especially when done in the presence of the management team. A large audacious meeting can be used for this purpose. Or a public memo serves nicely in a pinch.

A law firm I know used to circulate a memo each month, detailing the lawyers' billed hours. Ten first-year lawyers were stack ranked each month and could see where they were slotted from a performance perspective. Soon, many of the young lawyers began to work harder and longer hours to ascend the food chain more quickly. Eventually, lawyers could be found working evenings and Saturdays. It didn't take long to separate the top performers from the laggards.

On the flip side, public disclosure may humiliate rather than motivate some employees. That's why many firms prefer a private meeting between the manager and the employee where they can see how they rank.

Public-versus-private disclosure really depends on the mental makeup of your staff. With lawyers, they are competitive by nature, so the worst situation with stack ranking them is that the paramedics have to periodically show up to wheel out the ones who collapse from exhaustion. With more sensitive personalities, private disclosure is always best. Another aspect of private disclosure is that staff employees know that even though their co-workers don't see the rankings, the team leads, their VP and the CEO are aware of how they rank versus their peers.

Regardless of the method of disclosure, we have found the same productivity increase of 7% can be realized at all positions by stack ranking. For us, this 7% bounce has not diminished over the longer term. Once disclosure is made, everyone tries to increase their level of production as quickly as they can. What does that mean? Typically, with staff it means being more efficient, more innovative ideas, finishing projects faster, finding ways to eliminate wasted tasks and manage time more efficiently. This also focuses people to stay on task and off personal social-networking sites.

Sales forces are big users of the stack ranking. The increased productivity through competitiveness is usually instantaneous. Salespeople focus when the stack rankings are revealed, because the thought of "Sally Jo bringing in more business than me" will not be tolerated by competitive people who get paid on performance. Many times this tool guides the sales force to take their leads more seriously or make a few more phone calls per day to move up the stack. It also motivates the employees that want to be there, as well as inspiring your stars to widen the performance gap to remain on top.

A successful manager wants to weed out the low-performing salesman who is only collecting a paycheck in favor of paying the stars more for the enhanced performance. With stack ranking, you can accomplish this. Yet here's the best part about stack rankings: whatever metric you use to understand how well your employees are doing in their positions, it doesn't cost you one red cent. You don't have to bring in any motivational trainers or send your employees to another time management course.

Bold Knows Its Place and It Is on Top.

No cost to your company and one can add an additional 7% to the bottom line. What capitalistic company wouldn't do this to pull more revenue from its resources? Stack ranking suggests that providing information and feedback about employees' relative performance against their peers far surpasses numerous other efficiency metrics. That's how companies like yours crush it to Psycho Success.

CHAPTER FORTY-FIVE

Don't Be Pushed

Are you doing what someone else thinks your good at or are you following what excites you? I can't tell you how many friends I had growing up whose parents pushed them to follow a particular sport or career field, even though they were never really onboard with the choice. They literally wake up each day and long for a different life, not the one they were pushed into. At the end of the day, this is such a destructive and demoralizing process that it breaks you down physically and emotionally. Let's face it, if this is not your passion you may never truly succeed. The success you do achieve will never feel real, because it was never important to you. But typically, if you are not chasing your dream, success becomes tougher, as true dedication is not there. To be the best requires long hours and fervor or passion. Since you lack this obsessive behavior, you will never love what you're doing; success will never really materialize on so many levels. Your true dreams will never be realized.

Disapproval can be a strong lure to pursue the wrong path. Avoid this by getting involved in different groups and different activities. Consider traveling alone to really figure out where your passion lies. When you discover your true passion, then, and only then, can you concentrate your abilities in this career of choice.

This works for many MBA grads from Harvard who go to work on Wall Street. Their educators tell them to use the first two years out of college to explore their options while in New York, then select a chosen field. The point is their educators think it's in their best interest to take some time to understand where their real passion lies.

Bold Cannot Worry About What Others Think, Nor Can Bold Care.

Think about this: A man cannot directly choose his circumstances in this world, but can control his actions and thoughts to rise to a better life. It's all in your attitude and in your desire to climb to where you want to be. Find your passion and not what someone else wants for you.

CHAPTER FORTY-SIX

Psycho Pivot

There comes a time when every business begins to falter. If you are a startup seeking to be the next Twitter or Instagram or Facebook, there are literally tens of thousands of dead bodies lying around that had the same dream. For the smart ones that survive, they may not have become the next big thing, but they have great businesses. Whether your business is an online e-commerce company or a stump-grinding service, if you have been in business for the past couple of years, your business has probably seen better times. Maybe it's time to pivot.

Pivot is a buzzword Silicon Valley has given to startups when their original business model begins to fail, and they take the business in a whole new direction by doing something totally different from their original model. In the startup world, a team wants traction extremely fast or it wants to fail quickly so that it may use its remaining funding to pivot. Older companies can make this same pivot, but know it will be harder due to equipment, employees, relationships and other issues. But it has been done before. In fact, many private equity groups and corporate raiders do this. They will purchase a company and sell off the different assets or pieces of the company, and move forward with whatever portion of the business is most profitable, even though it may have been a subsidiary of the original business and was never a core business. That's why when your year-over-year growth on metrics is in steep decline, businesses need to take a moment to breathe, get creative and sometimes pivot. Execution is the key to pivoting successfully, but, then again, when is execution not important?

Bold Imagines the Future

and Finds the Blue Sky.

What are the assets or parts of my company that are making money? Where are we hemorrhaging? Stitch up the bleeding and sell off assets. Reset with whichever service or product has seen the most increased growth, most profit and most top-line revenue, or whichever metric is the most important to your business, and move forward. Take that part of the business and scale it, continuing to execute on the actions that have made that piece of the company a success.

Many times business owners have to detach themselves from their business, let someone else realize what is happening and make this decision for them. It's okay to not go down with the ship. Pivot and chart a new course in a new market. Is it tough to let go of old ways and take employees that may not have the skills to move forward in a new direction? Damn right! But better to pivot than lose your ass riding a business to bankruptcy.

Success is measured many ways in life. In business, the cash in your bank accounts commonly measures it, not by what business you are in. And getting that cash requires you to maintain high levels of productivity and profits for your company, regardless of the business model. How many businesses do you know of that are extremely strong, healthy and have plenty of resources, but are in the most mundane, unexciting and non-interesting trade on the planet? Yet each day they crush it for their families, employees and shareholders. It never ceases to amaze me when I come across companies that are highly successful with very wealthy owners, and I find out they make fan belts or a special hook for the women's girdle industry. Not exciting but effective. Ask those owners how many times they've had to change the course of their business or let employees go to move in a new direction and establish a new normal. I bet you'll be surprised at the pivot they made, which then made them a beast in their industry.

Don't be afraid to pivot. Every company will do it at some point. It may be subtle. It may be like making a U-turn with an aircraft carrier, but anything is better than swerving all over the road with no direction with a dying company and an outdated business model. Make the pivot decision and get back on top. Your employees and shareholders will love you for it. Pivots made with the right analytics and execution can be life changing. Bring the thunder in a pivot and Psycho Success will result.

CHAPTER FORTY-SEVEN

Productivity Rests

Coming from a tech background, I know that it can be tempting to try to power through the workday and long hours at the office. But your body's ability to focus truly only lasts about 90 minutes before you need to take a break. After 90 minutes, the brain literally has difficulty concentrating. Your body experiences physical restlessness. You become irritated and agitated easier. This is the danger zone where productivity can slip. Don't ignore signs from your body that you need a break in whatever task you are performing.

Many companies in the tech field have adopted a mandatory rest period of at least 20 minutes twice per day. To take this a step further, this may not include sleep, just basic rest and stepping away from what you have been doing over the previous period of time.

Remember, to execute at peak performance, focus your

energy on work in 90-minute cycles. This will help sustain your energy and allow focus during the entire day. Set a reminder every so often. Turn off your technology. Go for a walk. Read a fun article. Place a sign on the outside of your office - "Productivity Happens Here" - and do something different or simply take a power nap.

Even if you're crushing it and riding the good surf, put down what you are working on and do something else to rest your brain. Once you are rested and energized again, get back to your focused state and let the productivity flow more powerfully. I often find small mistakes when I dig back in, but these breaks from the action help keep me producing at a high level by being more focused on the current tasks of the day. Don't "Stay thirsty, my friends." For greater accomplishments through more focused productivity, "Stay rested, my friends." If your company is a leader, they'll get the concept. If not, be bold and show the bozos some serious results.

CHAPTER FORTY-EIGHT

Own the Inbox

Email marketing is a key component to the success of any business. Email marketing compliments your business online and off and enables you to reach people lightning quick. Typically, this could include customers you haven't met or done prior business with. Well-managed tech companies have email marketing and their email content management down to a science to promote more revenue. If you really do deep dives into well-run e-commerce companies, you'll find that they still believe owning the inbox is the best way to drive traffic and revenue through conversions to their sites.

Take Facebook or Twitter, for instance. They have long discovered the best way to find a customer and lead them back to their websites is through the inbox. Any time you are mentioned or tagged in a photo on either service you get a message sent directly to your inbox. Who doesn't want to see their photo or what someone said about them? So what does Joe Businessman or Joe Plumber do when he receives an email stating he has been tagged in a photo or that @sarahsays has mentioned him? He drops everything he is currently doing and clicks on the link in that email to find out what has become public domain. He cannot stand not to. No one can. People have to know immediately. In the process, they all drive traffic back to those sites for even more interaction, conversations and possible conversions. Not exactly Facebook's or Twitter's model, but essential for increased traffic never the less.

Any business can do this with a social component, but what if you don't have a social component to drive people to your website or storefronts? You incentivize and call customers to action through your short content and links in your promotional email messages. Examples could be: when you have a big sale, when an item gets marked down, when you host a party or meet-up or local speaker, or when you are giving away something free, send an email to your customers. Let them know your business has something worthwhile they are going to want to see. Many times you can send to those who have taken advantage of the offer in the email, so long as you have their permission. Celebrities in the community or well-known names are good examples of customers who can drive traffic and ultimately revenue. People tend to be followers, and "if it's good enough for Sally Celebrity, then it's good enough for me." Email marketing is no different. Own that inbox.

I have seen very successful companies send out 3-5 emails a day. Of course, they get many unsubscribes, but they also get people sharing the deal with their friends and the net effect is that the email list typically grows. But don't send an email just to fill someone's inbox. You need to have a deal or something important to say that affects the customer from an emotional perspective.

Don't Try to Be Clever. Be Clever.

The priority is to be always collecting emails. Make sure before people can use your website that you try to collect their email. If customers purchase something, send the receipt by email just to capture the address and to save a few trees. You can do this offline and inside your store at the point-of-purchase. You may even ask for their Twitter handle as well and occasionally send a shout out to them to stay atop the mindshare of your customers. If you do send an email blast out through a service, make sure it is an opt-in service and that every email you send has an unsubscribe link.

Although Search Engine Optimization (SEO) is important, I would certainly focus and budget more for acquisitions of email addresses and a content strategy with great calls to action. One more thing: SEO is always going to be about relevant content and highly rated sites linking back to your site. The only way to do this is through great and consistent press releases targeted specifically at your industry as well as influencers in your industry.

Business is a numbers game but has become much more targeted. As long as you can continue to grow your email address list and drive the subscribers back to your business with a specifically crafted content strategy centered on social contacts, you can keep these customers coming back through their inbox. Own the inbox and own a great company.

CHAPTER FORTY-NINE

Vanity's Metric

Anyone can put lipstick on a pig, spin a good story or toss up a measurable metric and release it to the world to show how great their company is. What some companies don't get is that a lot of these vanity metrics tossed to the press are nothing more than spin. They are intentionally skewing obscure numbers that have very little connection to the actual health or growth of the company. Of course, these metrics *do* make the company appear fantastic to the outside world, not to mention competitors.

Don't be afraid to use these vanity metrics in press releases or interviews to make your company look extraordinary and make your competitors sweat. The competition has no idea where these numbers truly came from. What they do get is the idea that your company is healthy, growing and crushing it in their same space. This *shock-and-awe* metrics tactic will have your competition think they are wallowing in their own slop, as they believe their product or company is lagging behind and nowhere near what your company has accomplished. Sometimes they'll panic and make crazy short-term business decisions that could further their company's decline.

Your competitors can't see all the knocks and pings under your hood but, instead, this monster truck heading right for them. You know there's still so much work to be done to be successful or go to market, or whatever the challenge your company is facing. Yet your competition has absolutely no idea your company is having issues. Everyone is under the perception that business is phenomenal, so when the competition thinks you are hammering them, it affects every resource they have, including, and most importantly, their employee morale.

With vanity metrics everything is always great in your company. That's the attitude you keep, and let it be known to the world. When perception is high, resources tend to be more abundant and so do clients.

In reality, you know that vanity metrics mean nothing; just something thrown over the fence to hurt the morale of your competition. This will happen repeatedly if these vanity metrics are periodically leaked to the press or publications. I know several tech companies whose employees believe the online news source TechCrunch or Mashable much more than they believe their own management. Why? Because it's in writing from an independent and valuable source of information on the Internet.

It's the cat and mouse playing games, but these games have real consequences for companies that don't understand how the game is played. The companies that can use these tactics correctly and efficiently will always lead the market from a perception standpoint. Who wouldn't want to do business with the market leader? Play the game. Don't get played in the press.

CHAPTER FIFTY

Gravy

I wanted to make the final chapter with important takeaways that hopefully stick in your head. So, here goes.

Total Anarchy

You are not in control of your company or brand or message any longer; the customer is. That is whom you report to. In today's age, you share your message with your audience through whatever channel you can. You craft the message but customers and society shape the story and how others perceive your company. Consumers project the perspective, and their perspective is the new reality. So understand all the angles that your message could take. Customers will even write your marketing message for you, if they really like your brand, but especially if they had an atrocious experience with your product or service. In short, your customers can make or break your business in a very short period of time. Don't shout marketing messages at your customer. Build on their conversation instead.

You Are Not Special

No matter how important you think you are to your company, you are replaceable, even if you own it. I see irreplaceable people replaced all the time and sometimes they have no idea. They have lost their social capital and may only hold the position, not the power.

You see it on sports teams. One big stud goes down or takes more money elsewhere for doing the same thing. Then the next man up fills the position—taking the team to even more elevated heights. An irreplaceable salesperson or CEO is caught in a scandal, gets sick or is in a car accident. Suddenly the company finds a replacement. Just like that. And the company actually survives without them. The second you think you are irreplaceable you lose your edge. You stop pushing, you stop fighting, and you take your foot off the gas. That's when you find out you *were* replaceable.

The Fringe Pays

Your customers are constantly engaged to information,

entertainment, conversations and social connections with people that matter to them. Your message needs to be where everyone is. To find out where everyone is, you must be everywhere. Everywhere is essential to your survival. Be available on every channel, including the fringe. You never know when your signal might pick up a paying customer with a large lifetime value upside.

10 Seconds

People are drowning in content everywhere. Messages are being lost. More video is uploaded to YouTube in 60 days than all three major U.S. networks produced in the last 60 years. And despite the fact that 60% of all Internet traffic now comes from video sites, 80% of people never get past the first 10 seconds. Think about that: 10 seconds is all you get to share your message. Be bold, be original and come out naked with your hair on fire if that's what it takes to catch your customer's attention.

Get Sick, Be Contagious

Content that "goes viral" is the kind of content that finds a place to live in your brain. It kicks you in the gut or makes you laugh. Perhaps you shed a tear. The content is talked about and passed around in social circles over and over. It takes creativity, getting to the point and some dumb luck messaging. Inspire, delight, entertain, shock, captivate and do whatever it takes to create an emotional experience that drives social participation. Remember, all it takes is one good sneeze to infect a large group of people.

Competition Doesn't Sleep

Ever have one of those dreams where the monster with the long claws is chasing you down and swiping at you? That monster is your competition. So how do you avoid this nightmare? Don't sleep. You can no longer go to sleep in this world. Your competition is always this close and wanting to kick your ass and take the market share that you have built. That share is yours and must be protected 24/7. Your company must be ready to react, respond and reach out at a moment's notice to avoid failure. Whatever you do, don't close your eyes.

The 401K Lever

If and when revenue and profits slow, you must think about ways to retain your employees, but lessen your company's burden to them. One way to do this is switch to a once-a-year 401(k) payment. Wall Street does this with bonuses, why not you? Currently, 84% of U.S. employers with 401(k) plans provide contributions every pay period, with only 9% providing annual, one-time, year-end payments. "More companies are now joining the once-a-year group," says *the Wall Street Journal.* Your company can set up a system where employees who leave before the last day of the year won't qualify for that year's 401(k) contribution. Nor will employees be able to benefit from interest or investment returns on the money throughout the year. The move could save thousands, if not millions, for your business. And the talent may think twice before they move on to greener pastures before December 31st.

CHAPTER FIFTY-ONE

Gravy with Biscuits

Even though I thought the last chapter was the final chapter, I decided to add one more bonus chapter with some unique thoughts that just might spark your imagination and some innovation in your company.

The Color of Creativity

Two groups in a research study were shown a two-second glimpse of a colored rectangle and then asked to complete a subsequent task of imagining various ways to use a small soda can. The first group was shown a green-colored rectangle, and the second group was shown a white one. "The first group demonstrated 20% more creativity than the second group," says a team led by Stephanie Lichtenfeld of the University of Munich in Germany. The researchers stated that in many cultures green has strong associations with growth and power. I would like to add that the color is also associated with: cash, money, loot, dough, Benjamins and scratch. Does this mean you should paint your company's offices green? Aren't we all going green these days?

Booing the Opposing Pitcher Delivers

"Baseball pitchers threw 40% fewer strikes when the crowd booed than when it cheered," according to an experiment led by L. Kimberly Epting of Elon University. Does this mean you should jeer your competition? Hammering your competitor whether online or in a business meeting will likely affect their performance in a substandard way. It's not a Jedi mind trick, it's just getting under their skin and just another way you can crush your competition. Sometimes you have to play the man, not the negotiation.

A Generous Relationship

It's common wisdom that you're more likely to make a sale if you build rapport with a client. Instead of focusing on the transaction, emphasize the connection by doing the following four things:

1. **Be generous.** Go into each meeting with a list of three

ways to make the prospect more successful. Don't worry about your return. Instead, think of it as good sales karma for which you may be rewarded.

2. Become a trusted advisor. Stay focused on your customer's success, not your quota.

3. Voice bold value. Only recommend your product when it's a great fit for their situation.

4. Believe in your ideas. If the ideas are simply explained, have a low barrier to entry with good upside for return, then you're much more likely to forge a trusting relationship with whomever you do business. Sorry, that may have been a layup.

What Recession?

The recession challenged many long-held rules about how to boost revenue. Instead of slashing prices and cutting customer support, *invest* in customer support. Because the next level of new revenue often comes from renewals, additions, up sells and maintenance. Double down on your focus for after-the-sale-service and kick-ass customer support. This will keep customers coming back, because the investment should yield a very good user experience. Try to hold the line on your price points and margins and never give your product away unless it's a loss leader for an item or a service with far larger margins. Compete on friendly service and your unique difference—not the depth of your discounts. If you can hold out long enough, many of your competitors will disappear due to taking the opposite approach.

To Get Further, Go for the Head

"Powerful people who were asked their height, judged themselves to be an average of six inches taller in comparison to people in lower social positions," said Michelle M. Duguid of Washington University and Jack A. Goncalo of Cornell. According to the researchers, being physically elevated makes a person feel powerful and seem influential to others. Powerful people think they are more impressive if they can peer over their laptops and boost their supreme brilliance. In reality, it clearly masks their insecurities but whatever the case, compliment your clients on their appearance and height in a casual conversation and have a contract ready.

Make It a Headline Tomorrow

Clear and well-articulated presentations are always a great listen, but they won't necessarily be remembered. Be relevant and memorable by using great quotes or sound bites recorded earlier. These sound bites get picked up and repeated and lead to larger memory share. Rhythmic repetition is also a big help. Repeat a keyword or phrase at the beginning, middle or end of your sentences. Use these rhetorical speech patterns throughout the presentation, and people will walk away remembering your catchy word or phrase and hopefully your name. Piggyback on the familiar. Take something most people know and make it your own. Spin-offs of the "Got Milk?" slogan have done this very successfully. Deliver a repeatable, concise and memorable statement; it may just be the headline tomorrow.

Disrupt

In the movie *Cool Hand Luke,* the warden, known as "the Captain," tells prisoner Paul Newman: "You're gonna get your mind right, Luke." With this book, I want to get your mind right. That means throwing out old ways of thinking. Leave the reality and rethink how you could disrupt your market or the interaction in the market. Go from film to the digital world. Move from faxing to direct messaging. Hang up the landline and go hands-free mobile. If you want to achieve Psycho Success, you have to get your mind right and that means seeing the future, disrupting the norm and kicking your competition's ass.

Bold Is Beginning to Change You.

Dent the Universe

As a reminder, disseminate your bold. Let your freak flag fly and celebrate it. Bold is broadcast by savvy aptitude and venturing differently. On resolution alone Bold is successful. This is due to Bold's confidence, certainty and tenaciousness. Everyone likes and speaks about Bold, but others don't have the fortitude or the slant to be Bold. Bold uses intelligence as it goes for the throat in business. Bold networks on the fringe, cultivating relationships others would not and is relevant in any conversation by detonating the box.

Bold is not ashamed of his past, his irregular foresight or his overwhelming success. Bold wants the exposure, the attention that moves his agenda, because Bold knows it communicates uncommon value. Bold leads, doesn't wait, doesn't slow and shows zero fear. Fear keeps Bold on the fast break, a step ahead and in favor with the Lord. It took a Bold stroke to create this world, and Bold is handsomely rewarded today as it is on a higher plain. In today's vernacular, Bold is the new black, but truly it should be the light that propels you to dent the universe.

Bring the Thunder,

Mattox

About the Author

After several corporate sales positions and numerous business failures, Mattox is today a Psycho Successful entrepreneur. He has founded and funded numerous startups and businesses over his 20-year career. He is a technology generalist, e-commerce expert and advisor to several startups that are out to dent the universe. He is a motivational speaker and an inspiration to audiences, having battled a speech impediment since a young age.

He is always looking for new and exciting business opportunities that allow him to carry forward his "Bold Is" attitude. Contact him with your opportunity on twitter @psychosuccess or by email at mattox@psychosuccess.com for speaking engagements or with your business opportunities.

www.ingramcontent.com/pod-product-compliance
Lightning Source LLC
Chambersburg PA
CBHW051520170526
45165CB00002B/544